Mixed Method Design

Developing Qualitative Inquiry

Series Editor: Janice Morse
University of Utah

Books in the new **Developing Qualitative Inquiry** series, written by leaders in qualitative inquiry, will address important topics in qualitative methods. Targeted to a broad multidisciplinary readership, the books are intended for midlevel/advanced researchers and advanced students. The series will forward the field of qualitative inquiry by describing new methods, or developing particular aspects of established methods.

Series Editorial Board: H. Russell Bernard, Kathy Charmaz, D. Jean Clandinin, Julianne Cheek, Juliet Corbin, Carmen de la Cuesta, John Engel, Sue E. Estroff, Jane Gilgun, Jeffrey C. Johnson, Joe Maxwell, Carl Mitcham, Katja Mruck, Judith Preissle, Jean J. Schensul, Sally Thorne, John van Maanen, Max van Manen

Volumes in this series:

1. Autoethnography as Method, *Heewon Chang*
2. Interpretive Description, *Sally Thorne*
3. Developing Grounded Theory: The Second Generation, *Janice M. Morse, Phyllis Noerager Stern, Juliet Corbin, Barbara Bowers, Kathy Charmaz,* and *Adele E. Clarke*
4. Mixed Method Design, *Janice M. Morse* and *Linda Niehaus*

MIXED METHOD DESIGN

Principles and Procedures

Janice M. Morse and Linda Niehaus

Walnut Creek, California

LEFT COAST PRESS, INC.
1630 North Main Street, #400
Walnut Creek, CA 94596
http://www.LCoastPress.com

ISBN 978-1-59874-297-8 hardcover
ISBN 978-1-59874-298-5 paperback

Library of Congress Cataloging-in-Publication Data

Morse, Janice M.
Mixed method design : principles and procedures / Janice M. Morse, Linda Niehaus.
    p. cm.—(Developing qualitative inquiry)
Includes bibliographical references and index.
ISBN 978-1-59874-297-8 (hardcover : alk. paper)—ISBN 978-1-59874-298-5 (pbk. : alk. paper)
1. Social sciences—Research—Methodology. 2. Social sciences—Statistical methods.
3. Qualitative research. 4. Quantitative research. I. Niehaus, Linda. II. Title.
H62.M6611 2009
300.72—dc22 2009021214

Printed in the United States of America

⊗™ The paper used in this publication meets the minimum requirements of American
National Standard for Information Sciences—Permanence of Paper for Printed Library
Materials, ANSI/NISO Z39.48–1992.

09 10 11 12 13   5 4 3 2 1

Contents

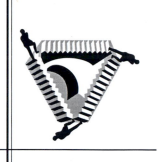

Dedication

*To Bob: who listens, critiques, and reads
and reminds me that life transcends method*
—Jan

*To Aimee: my little dog, who is supportive in her
unconditional love and patience*
—Linda

List of Illustrations

Figures

Tables

Preface

Roadmap: Before you read this book . . .

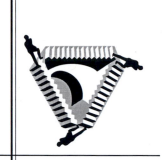

Mixed methods is the latest approach to social science research—so new we have barely decided what it is (Johnson, Onwuegbuzie, & Turner, 2007), under what conditions to use it, how to do it, and what rules ensures its legitimacy. In response to this gap—and the demand for the method—a number of books have recently been published about mixed methods (Bergman, 2008; Greene, 2007; Creswell & Plano Clark, 2007; Ridenour & Newman, 2008; Teddlie & Tashakkori, 2009), including a *Sage Handbook* (Tashakkori & Teddlie, 2003), a quarterly journal (*Journal of Mixed Methods Research*), many articles, (Greene 2005; 2006; Maxwell, 2007; Morgan, 1998) and collections of research (see, for example, Bryman, 2006a; Plano Clark & Creswell, 2008).

Do we need another book?

Despite all this enthusiasm from researchers, educational programs, granting agencies, and graduate students, no one has written a book about how to actually do it. Researchers who have tried to determine methodological rules by analyzing articles or interviewing researchers have identified something very interesting. After analyzing 232 articles, Bryman (2006b, 2007, 2008) noted that "integration of mixed-methods is not achieved and is difficult to do" (p. 95). Interviews with 20 researchers revealed that: (1) the kinds of questions that mixed methods best addresses have not been identified; (2) nomenclature has not been completely developed; and (3) there is "little in the way of prescriptive writing on doing mixed method research"; of greatest concern, when asked to identify one exemplar of mixed methods "virtually all of the interviewees struggled with the question" (Bryman, 2008, p. 98).

In this book, we will try to fill some of these gaps by explicating mixed method research design, primarily focusing on mixed method designs that use both qualitative and quantitative methods. We will also discuss mixed methods design when you are using both quantitative and qualitative strategies. *Mixed methods design refers to the use of two (or more) research methods in a single study, when one (or more) of the methods is not complete in itself.* That is, we define mixed methods as the incorporation of one or more methodological strategies, or techniques drawn from a second method, into a single research study, in order to access some part of the phenomena of interest that cannot be accessed by the use of the first method alone. The use of mixed method design makes the study more comprehensive or complete than if a single method was used.

Mixed method research is therefore a systematic way of using two or more research methods to answer a single research question. It includes using two (or more) qualitative or quantitative methods or it uses *both* qualitative and quantitative methods. The latter combination of qualitative and quantitative methods is the most difficult, because mixing paradigms means that the researcher is using contradictory assumptions and rules for inquiry. The goal is to retain maximum validity while adhering to the rules inherent in each paradigm. The trick is to realize what rules of inquiry may or may not be broken or compromised, to foresee the ramifications of breaking rules, and to recognize how to compensate for these problems.

Mixed method designs are NOT a *blending* of research methods. We do not collect data in a willy-nilly fashion and then try to think of a way to combine it in the analysis so we can "see what we have got." Mixed method designs are not, as we have heard them described, like a stir fry, a collection of nuts, or a more expensive drink. (Maxwell [2007] notes that "mixed" really has "misleading connotations," but it is too late to change it.) Rather, mixed method designs are planned, rigorous, and—although challenging to conduct—provide very strong, publishable research findings. They are exciting to do, rewarding, and often produce results that are broader and of more significant impact than research that uses one method alone.

Why This Book?

Our intention is to produce clear and unfettered principles for conducting mixed method research, remove the pitfalls of combining divergent research methods, and make the processes logical and clear. As a researcher, once you understand what, why, and when a research strategy is needed to collect data that will provide a certain kind of information, most of the risk in doing mixed method research is removed. Research is a deliberate process, with well-developed rules for inquiry. Once you are aware of these rules, when they should be followed and, if violated, what the consequences are, then as threats to validity are diminished, researcher anxiety is reduced, and your research becomes as fascinating and as interesting as it should be.

Sound dogmatic? Some will label our approach as "parallel." That's ok. We hope that others will build on this foundation. At least this is a start.

How new is mixed method design? Mixed method design is a name given to research practices that have actually been conducted for decades. For instance, the multiple sources of data in ethnographic research are standard components ethnographic design. Despite this, ethnography is just considered ethnography—it is not usually considered a mixed method, yet the combination of multiple methodological strategies or techniques is what makes "ethnography" ethnography. If a research study is comprised of two components and both components are "complete"—that is, they could be published separately in their own right, we do not call this mixed method, but rather "multiple method" design. A multiple method design is a plan for a research program comprised of two or more related scientifically rigorous research projects conducted over time. Both mixed and multiple method designs have been known as triangulated designs; they have been used for a long time. Researchers argue that exploring a phenomenon from two or more perspectives provides more information than one used alone, with the different methods compensating for deficiencies in the other. They also argue that one set of findings validates (confirms) the other. Occasionally, mixed method studies are difficult to identify, as researchers tend to gloss over strategies that may be considered by reviewers to be incomplete. Alternatively, with multiple method design, researchers tend to publish each of the studies in separate journals, sometimes not even referring to other related studies, so that the multiple studies that make the research program appear in various journals, occasionally punctuated with review articles summarizing the progress in the research.

Mixed methods have been used by more daring researchers for decades, with quantitative researchers, for instance, using qualitative interviews to identify items for their questionnaires and to explain unexpected findings or unanticipated results, and qualitative researchers using quantitative measures to enrich their descriptions and even to "test" their models or theories.

One consequence of the recent interest in mixed method designs is a scramble among researchers to develop notation and to identify designs so that different researchers are using different terms for different components and developing contradictory rules. Even deciding what a mixed method study is and what it is not causes consternation and disagreement. Therefore, we have provided a list of definitions used in this book (see Appendix 1) and hope that we are at least being clear and consistent in the use of our terms.

Applying terminology to components of research designs that already exist makes us feel rather like the early anatomists. Instead of labeling the body, we are analyzing research designs, mapping or diagramming them, and then applying "maps" we develop to other studies to see if they work in other cases or if other research designs are explicated using this system. In the process of developing this system, we have conducted workshops with students and researchers from many disciplines, listened to their concerns and frustrations, and tried to clarify and simplify what they were doing and to diagram their designs. We hope you find our terminology and schemas useful also.

This book is largely about the most difficult of mixed method designs—using qualitative and quantitative methods within the same study. We devote a small section to studies using two different qualitative methods and to studies mixing two quantitative designs—the easiest of all mixed methods designs.

We assume that those using this book have had at least one course on qualitative methods and one course on quantitative methods. If you do not have this background, you may find it difficult to understand this book and will need to read it with your basic books at hand. Some readers, we know, will be working in research teams, with some team members being experts in qualitative and some in quantitative inquiry. We hope that the principles we present here will make sense to researchers from both paradigms and that they will be able to wisely negotiate a solid mixed method design.

What Is "Mixed"?

With the renewed interest in mixed methods, explicating mixed method design is still immature and at the stage where there is some scrambling for terminology and establishing the rules for rigor; there is still some uncertainty regarding the "rules." One such discussion centers on the question of whether mixed methods are parallel methods or truly meshed. We take a middle ground. Our two methods meet at the points of interface and are conducted separately between. Actually, we cannot think of a single example that is both meshed and valid! Our colleagues ask which method is *dominant*—and we answer that we do not like that term (nor do we like *priority*). *Theoretical drive* is a better term; it implies the guiding of the research project, rather than one method being "better" than the other. We answer that the theoretical drive used depends on the research question, the type of inquiry, and the level of the research program. Either qualitative or quantitative may "drive," and we have made this explicit in the concepts of *theoretical drive* and *theoretical thrust*. One method must always drive: We cannot think of a single study with "equivalent design." And once one discards the notion of *equivalence*, life in the research design arena becomes much easier.

There are some areas of agreement: Most researchers now agree mostly on the major types of designs. However, we still have trouble with the designs that place the supplemental strategy first. Such projects have nothing to build on and, again, we could not find an example of such a project in the literature. Creswell and Plano Clark (2007) have another design that troubles us: *embedded* design, in which a project is encompassed within another project. To us, embedded design makes no sense. Research studies *always* contribute some knowledge. Why conduct a study that you are going to ignore, submerge, and makes no contribution to the results?

Is mixed method design difficult? We hope not. We do it and have done it for a long time. We have conducted many workshops on this method, and participants appear to go away less confused, sometimes even "seeing the light." We have published portions of these methods and we have had the satisfaction of seeing some of our terminology and principles accepted and appearing in the work of others. We hope, now that this book has put it all together, that the field will move forward with one voice, and at least some of the scrambling, uncertainty, and discussion will shift to truly tricky and thorny issues, which are more worthy of our attention.

But we are getting ahead of ourselves—let us discuss how this book is organized. Following a general introduction in Chapter 1, the main components of mixed method design will be presented in Chapter 2, with theoretical drive, pacing of component(s), and the point of interface introduced in Chapters 3–5. Sampling is discussed in Chapter 6. The issues of planning a project are found in Chapter 7—before the in-depth discussion of the major designs—so you will be aware of the most pressing issues as you read Chapter 8, Qualitatively-Driven Designs and Chapter 9, Quantitatively-Driven Designs. In Chapter 10, we present complex designs, including mixed and multiple method research programs. We have placed basic information in the Appendices: Appendix I includes a compendium of terms; Appendix II includes a worksheet for analyzing mixed method studies; and Appendix 3 provides information for library searching for mixed method studies.

This book was a long time in the writing stage, and we are grateful for the help we have received along the way. We thank the students at the IIQM (International Institute for Qualitative Methodology), EQUIPP program, who were enthusiastically engaged in mixed methods as we developed our thinking—in particular, Seanne Wilkins, Ruth Wolfe, Kim Deschamps, Katharyn Weaver, and other graduate students from the mixed methods classes at the University of Alberta. Linda Slater, University of Alberta John Scott Health Science Library, assisted with literature searches and has contributed Appendix III describing the use of search engines for mixed method research. Mitch Allen, Editor-in-Chief, Left Coast Press, was the driving force moving this book from conception to your shelf—thank you!

Janice M. Morse
Linda Niehaus

1

Mixed Method Design: Who Needs It?

I hate the term mixed method. *It sounds like a salad!*
　　—David Maines, personal communication, 2008

When a researcher asks a question that cannot be answered using a single method, the research outcome may be improved by using more than that one method. This occurs when the phenomenon is complex or when, for instance, the researcher wants to explore a question at the macro- (e.g., the group) level as well as at the micro- (e.g., individual) level and researchers need to describe both minutely and globally. Alternatively, the researcher may wish to explore different aspects of the same phenomenon, such as the experience and the behavioral response, or develop a research design that will allow us to simultaneously understand mechanisms, explore associations, and document risks. To grasp complex phenomenon, research often demands that more than one research method be used in the same project. Consequently, researchers must be versatile and adept at many types of research and research methods, both qualitative and quantitative.

The obvious way to address such complexities in research may be to conduct more than one research project, each using a different method. Using two complete methods for conducting two scientifically rigorous research projects over time, that is, *multiple method research*, clearly takes twice as long and costs twice as much as a single project, and requires twice the skills. Instead, you may choose to conduct a single project and include a supplemental component by using a strategy drawn from a second, different method for collecting or analyzing the data that will enhance the description, understanding or explanation of the phenomenon under investigation. Although such a supplemental component is not complete enough to stand alone and be published separately, it is a viable compromise because it provides you with adequate answers and enough confidence to move forward with your research. Such a research design,

> Multiple method research program is a series of complete related qualitative and/or quantitative *research projects*, driven by the *theoretical thrust* of the program.

consisting of one core component with an additional supplementary component that fits into the core component of the study, is defined as *mixed method research*. The defining characteristic of mixed method research is that it involves a primary or core method combined with one or more strategies drawn from a second, different method for addressing the research question by either collecting or analyzing data. The supplemental component is partially complete and not conducted rigorously enough to stand alone or to be published by itself.

> A mixed method design is a scientifically rigorous *research project*, driven by the inductive or deductive *theoretical drive*, and comprised of a qualitative or quantitative *core component* with qualitative or quantitative *supplementary component(s)*.

Mixed method research often (but not always) involves the use of both qualitative and/or quantitative methods. For instance, a mixed method design might entail the use of a qualitative method (to describe some experience, for example) with an additional quantitative strategy to a measure some dimension of the experience. Measuring a dimension of this experience enriches the qualitative description of the phenomenon under investigation. Alternatively, a quantitative method might be used to measure some experience, and a qualitative strategy may be added to the research design to allow for description of an aspect of the phenomenon that cannot be measured and that would enhance the narrative description of the phenomenon.

A mixed method design, if conducted with deliberate care, is a stronger design than one that uses a single method because the supplemental component enhances validity of the project per se by enriching or expanding our understanding or by verifying our results from another perspective (see, for example, Locke, Silverman, & Spirduso, 1998, p. 117; Onwuegbuzie & Johnson, 2006). Further, with mixed method designs all components remain intact and are published as a whole, as one study, whereas in multiple method design the researchers often publish each study separately in a different journal, without even citing the other related study(ies), so that the hard-earned comprehensiveness of the research program is lost. Mixed method studies also may not be without a downside, for Morgan (2004) has noted that on occasions the supplemental component of the mixed method design, because of its incompleteness, may be criticized by reviewers as being weak, unsound, or even lacking rigor, and may be the cause for the rejection of the article.

Advantages of Mixed Method Design

Is conducting a mixed method design, rather than a multiple method design, cutting corners, compromising quality for convenience? Should not all designs exploring complex phenomena use multiple methods, with all components of the design employing complete and rigorous methods in order to study the phenomenon most comprehensively? The answer to these questions is that there is a role for mixed method design: It enables the completion of a single research project more expeditiously and efficiently than conducting a multiple methods design that entails a series of related research projects conducted over time. The supplemental component of a mixed methods design is regarded as complementary to the core component of the project, providing answers of adequate quality, so that researchers may progress with their research with certainty.

Mixed method design is the easiest to conduct when both the core and the supplemental components are from the same paradigm—both are qualitative components or both quantitative components. We discuss these designs in Chapters 8 and 9—and although they are the easiest, they are also the least common, possibly because many do not consider combining two methods from the same paradigm as mixed methods.

> The *core component* of the project is the complete method used to address the research question.

The Purpose of Mixed Method Designs

The exploratory nature of research, the complexities of the phenomena studied in social science, and the limitations within methods means that there are occasions when a phenomenon cannot be described in its entirety using a single method. Sometimes, to comprehensively address the research question, a project using both qualitative and quantitative methods must be proposed. At other times, unexpected findings emerge that demand to be addressed during the course of a project. Sometimes these findings may best be addressed using another methodological strategy. For instance, in a qualitatively-driven project, a need for *measurement* of certain aspects of the phenomenon may arise, demanding the use of a quantitative strategy. Similarly, during a quantitatively-driven project, surprising findings that occur during the analysis may indicate the need for additional description using a qualitative strategy, such as interviews, to be conducted. Such possibilities mean that, to complete the study, a mixed method design must be used. This approach would incorporate a supplementary component that may or may not have been anticipated at the proposal stage.

> The *supplementary component* is a methodological strategy different from the method, use to extend investigation. The supplementary component is incomplete in itself or lacks some aspect of scientific rigor, *cannot stand alone* and is regarded as complementary to the core component.

Who uses mixed methods? They are used when the phenomena being studies is considered complex and beyond the reach of a single method. The growing popularity of mixed methods research has extended into policy (Caracelli, 2006), evaluation (Chen, 2006; Greene, Benjamin, & Goodyear, 2001), education (Greene, 2006; Rocco et al., 2003), management and organizational research (Currall & Towler, 2003), psychology (Todd et al., 2004), medicine—mainly in primary care (Creswell, Fetters, & Ivankova, 2004), family medicine (Borkan, 2004; Sussman et al., 2006), and psychiatry (Wittink, Barg, & Gallo, 2006), nursing (Twinn, 2003), health services (Johnstone, 2004), and health promotion (Campbell et al., 2000; Milburn et al., 1995). Mixed methods have been used in international aging research (Curry, Shield, & Wetle, 2006), to combine qualitative research with randomized trials (Donavan et al., 2002), to measure change (Hroscikoski et al., 2006), interaction (Ridenour & Newman (2008), or for building theory (Morgan & Stewart, 2002). Johnson and Onwuegbuzie (2004, p. 14) note it is a new research paradigm—the third paradigm—whose "time has come."

What Is a "Good" Mixed Method Design Research Question?

We have said that mixed method studies should be used for complex aims or questions but have not explained how to recognize a complex aim and subsequently the questions that require a mixed method design. Let's start with a simple question and work from there:

What is a simple research question? Simple questions are usually clear cut, so that an easy design may be identified directly from the question. For instance:

- The researcher is only interested in one group, or the comparison of one dimension/variable set when comparing two or more groups.
- The question does not involve change or trajectories, multiple measures, or experimental design.
- The research involves a single concept, one that is well developed and easily measured.
- The research should involve a narrow-targeted, unidimensional question, one that is easily represented in the research design.
- The research consists of a single data type.

Mixed Method Simultaneous Design

Mixed method simultaneous designs are projects in which the core and the simultaneous projects are conducted at the same time. In contrast to a simple question, *if* a study is at the planning stages and the researcher has to address a complex research aim or question, a simultaneous mixed method design could be identified when:

- the study has multiple groups of participants (compares different roles [students/teachers; patients/caregivers], occupations [physicians/nurses]) and so forth;
- the study contains several types of variables that do not "fit" well together in the analytic scheme (e.g., physiological, behavioral, psychological/emotional);
- the process of documenting changes the phenomenon itself or the trajectory, over time, has multiple data points, and sometimes even the phenomenon itself changes (the "butterfly phenomenon") so that even the modes of measurement must change with the phenomenon;
- different components of interest within a setting demand different types of data to be collected (e.g., documents, actors, actions);
- multiple dimensions of a concept, or several concepts and/or variables demand to be considered using different forms of measurement;

> Simultaneous mixed method designs are those in which the core and the supplementary component are conducted at the same time.

- complex concepts (i.e., historical, value-laden, abstract) are combined with concrete phenomena;
- a theory may have various concepts and different types of outcome variables;
- there is a broad, encompassing question, rather than a narrow, targeted question.

Mixed Method Sequential Design

Doing the supplemental component after the completion of the core component would be a sequential design. If the core component has been completed, the sample used in the core component is usually no longer available, so the researcher is forced to draw another sample from the sample population according to the needs of the supplemental component (see Sampling, Chapter 6).

> Sequential mixed method designs are those in which the supplementary component are conducted after the core has been completed.

Sequential mixed method designs are those projects in which the supplemental project is conducted after the core project has been completed. It is usually designed at the proposal stage; however, *if* the study has been underway for a period of time and new questions emerge, or if the analysis of the project is completed and the researcher wishes to resolve some question about the unexpected findings, then an *emergent* mixed methods design is used.

Emergent design is a study in which the supplementary component is added *after* the core component of the study is underway or completed and the researcher realizes that the present study is inadequate and that additional information—or answering a supplemental question—would greatly improve the research. An emergent design, therefore, is a sequential design that was not planned at the proposal stage. It is possible to answer the question while the project is ongoing, if, of course, you have a simultaneous design.

> Emergent design is a project that is added after the core component is underway or completed.

Adding a component when the core study is underway means that the researcher must obtain ethical clearance from his or her institutional review board and, if the study is a doctoral dissertation, also from his or her supervisory committee. The other awkward consideration is the additional funding necessary for the supplementary component and permission from the funding organization. Although these tasks take time, if the study can be completed as a mixed method study, the researcher is generally ahead in terms of his or her research program rather than proposing and conducting a separate study in a multiple method design.

What a Mixed Methods Design Is and Is Not

What is a mixed method design study? We have already listed the most important defining characteristic:

Mixed method design consists of a core component (the main, scientifically rigorous study in which the primary or core method is used) and a supplemental component that is not complete in itself within which one or more strategies drawn from another method is used. This means that both components of mixed method research must always be published as one article. Although researchers may be tempted to publish each study from a multiple method research program in two different journals, mixed method researchers do not have that option. As the supplemental component is "incomplete," it only has meaning, or significance, in the context of the core component, and is not rigorous enough to be published alone.

Now consider what a mixed method study is *not*:

- A mixed method study is *not* a quantitative study that contains several variables, each measured with different instruments. Although this is a very common design for a quantitative study, all of these instruments (and variables) comprise a part of the core study.
- A mixed method project is *not* a pilot study followed by the main study (*quan*—>QUAN). A pilot study preceding the main study is a common design intended to evaluate various aspects of the study that will be used in the main study. The pilot study and the main study are both parts of the same entity.
- A mixed method study is *not* a study consisting of a qualitative component (such as qualitative interviews or focus groups) that is used for the purpose of developing items for the instrument that will be developed in the main study. This qualitative component is a normal part of instrument development and *not* a *qual*—>QUAN design.
- A mixed method design is *not* the quantitative description of the sample that normally precedes every study, including a qualitative study.
- Mixed method design is *not* a quantitative questionnaire with a single open-ended question at the end. This is so common that it may be considered a normal part of questionnaires. Including a single open-ended question does not make the study a mixed method design study, and this design *cannot* be described as being a quantitative and qualitative mixed design.
- Some qualitative methods, by definition, consist of several data sources. For example, ethnography consists of interviews, participant observation field notes, a diary, and other data sources—maps, kinship analyses, psychometric measurements, or anything else that may be pertinent to the question. Although ethnography is truly a mixed method design (and may be considered a qualitatively-driven mixed method design), it is not listed as such because it is these various methodological approaches to studying culture that makes ethnography "ethnography." Ethnography has become so institutionalized and eclectic that, in fact, its very flexibility is one of the

characteristics that defines it as one complete method. Similarly, if you are doing grounded theory by interviewing and observing both of those data collection strategies are part of grounded theory and do not make it a mixed method design.

- Let us consider the contribution of the *supplementary component*. Ideally, for a study to be considered mixed method, each component must contribute to the study theoretically—it cannot simply be a strategy, for instance, to enable measurement. The supplemental component has to enhance description, understanding, or explanation of the phenomenon under investigation.

Sometimes when we are reading mixed method design, we find that the researchers have completed a series of studies and they are really working as a multiple method design. And indeed there is some confusion in the literature—some authors call multiple method design mixed method design and do not make the distinction between mixed and multiple method designs. However, because mixed method design is so complex, we think this distinction is important.

At times when we are reading mixed method studies, we find that the author claims to have used a mixed method design and may even describe the design correctly. But when we read the results, we find the researcher has presented the results only from the core component (either the qualitative or the quantitative) and has ignored the supplemental component. Morgan (1998) writes that because the supplemental component is incomplete, reviewers tend to be critical of these components. Some authors may think, albeit incorrectly, that the article is stronger and more likely to be accepted if it is not submitted as a mixed method study and the supplemental component is omitted from the manuscript.

Current Debates in Mixed Methods

Discussions, disagreements, and divergences abound in mixed methods manuals. We hope that it is simply an artifact of the newfound interest in mixed methods, and we approach this section with some trepidation. Our initial impulse was to skip it altogether, but dodging is also a practice that can be criticized.

The difficulty with mixed method projects is that qualitative and quantitative research have been described as belonging to different—and incompatible—paradigms (Greene, 2006), so *how* the researcher combines the qualitative and the quantitative components in a single project is an essential consideration if rigor is to be maintained. This "incompatibility" problem is at the heart of the discussions about mixed methods. Borkan (2004) notes that some of these problems may have to with "academic turf." Much of this concern lies with the possible disciplinary devaluation of the qualitative component (Creswell et al., 2006) or the devaluation of anything less than experimental designs (Denzin & Lincoln, 2005).

Another problem is that there is no consensus about how to evaluate mixed method designs. Some authors recommend using both qualitative and quantitative criteria for evaluating mixed methods (e.g., Sale & Brazil, 2004); others note that validity is a critical issue beyond the sum of its parts—to the extent that Onwuegbuzie & Johnson (2006) propose a new term for validity: *legitimation.*

How do you define mixed methods? Our colleagues even have disagreement regarding this, and in 2007, Johnson, Onwuegbuzie, and Turner addressed the issue head on and phoned all of the major players for their definition. Most of the researchers in this study agreed that it was qualitative and quantitative methods that were mixed; we agree that that combination is the most difficult, but that a mixed method design may also mix two qualitative methods or two quantitative methods. Our definition of mixed methods is that the study consists of a qualitative or quantitative core component and a supplementary component (which consists of qualitative or quantitative research strategies but is not a complete study in itself). The research question dictates the theoretical drive, as either inductive or deductive, so that the onus is on the researcher to be versatile and competently switch inductive and deductive positions according to the need of the study. A part of what is and is not a mixed method design is the pacing of the components and their interaction. We have presented our view—it appears to work, appears to pass present validity tests, and gets one to where one is trying to go.

Our Perspective:

- Mixed methods and multiple methods are not the same, but are two distinct approaches. Of these two, mixed methods is the most difficult.

- Design must be developed logically and optimally from the research question.

- Neither the qualitative nor the quantitative are "privileged" with one method consistently dominant over the other. Which method is dominant depends on the question and the theoretical drive of the study. In this book, we have ordered our sections by discussing qualitative methods first, before quantitative, for no particular reason except qualitative usually precede quantitative for some types of inquiry and for the sake of neurotic consistency.

- The research methods must be conducted separately, in parallel until the point of interface.

Principles of Mixed Method Design

Although we are still working to develop agreement on the *best way* to do mixed method design, we propose some principles that will, at least minimally, assist you to retain validity. We will return to these principles throughout the book.

Table 1.1 Principles of mixed method design

Principle #1:	Work with as few data sets as possible (or, keep it simple!).
Principle #2:	The more you know about research methods, the easier mixed methods will be!
Principle #3:	Recognize and respect the project's theoretical drive.
Principle #4:	Recognize the role of the supplemental component.
Principle #5:	Adhere to the methodological assumptions of each method.
Principle #6:	Carefully consider the pacing of the components.
Principle #7:	Sampling must be compatible with the assumptions belonging to the method or strategy it serves.
Principle #8:	Mixed method design is systematic.
Principle #9:	Keep the two data sets separate until the point of interface.
Principle #10:	Adhere to the methodological assumptions of the core method.
Principle #11:	The direction of the theoretical drive is evident in the core component. But between the supplemental sample selection and the point of interface, the researcher must adhere to the paradigmatic assumptions of the supplemental method.
Principle #12:	If you can measure, measure. Just keep any limitations in mind.
Principle #13:	Whatever is being coded and/or counted must make sense.

Ideally, to conduct mixed method design research, the researcher has to be "methodologically versatile." Researchers *should* be very experienced and knowledgeable in both qualitative and quantitative methods—or lucky enough to have a wise, research-smart, dissertation supervisor. Failing that, throughout this book we will provide you with principles that will make the process of conducting mixed method research slightly less perilous.

> Principle 1: Work with as few data sets as possible (or, keep it simple!)

Your first thought about mixed methods is correct. A mixed method study is almost twice the work (and certainly twice the worry) of a single method study. The researcher has to gain skills in both the primary method and the strategies drawn from the second method, supervise research assistants (or become adept oneself) at using multiple data collection and/or analysis strategies, and have the wisdom to see the relevance, pertinence, and essential need of these strategies.

The truth is mixed method design can consist of as many supplemental components (i.e., the second strategy that makes the mixed method mixed) as one wishes in a single project (we will not return to this unpleasant fact until Chapter 10, Complex Designs). Every time you add a supplementary component, you add a new dimension of work and new aspects threatening the validity of your study. Before adding a supplementary component, a wise researcher does a cost-benefit analysis and an armchair walkthrough, asking "Will these results be worth the effort?" Remember: "Parsimony is perfection" and "mixed method design" is easier to say than do! And remember: *Always know what you are doing and why!* If you are not confident with using a method, find a mentor, or a competent co-investigator, or consultant, or stick with and accept the limitations of using a single-method design. Others have done so before and have even received their degree.

2

The Nuts and Bolts of Mixed Method Design

Aim to become an expert methodologist in both qualitative and quantitative inquiry. The trick is to be able to select the best methods to answer your research question(s), to be able to recognize what is possible given your methodological toolbox, and to be alert to (and avoid) all possible pitfalls. Our goal is that you reach your research goal without compromising the quality of your research.

In this chapter, we will give you a "feel for" the basics of mixed method design. We are aware that we are introducing a lot of new terminology all at once, and will define terms as we go along, but you may wish to consult the glossary in Appendix I. Here, we will discuss considerations for conducting mixed method research and later discuss basic mixed method designs.

> Principle #2: The more you know about research methods, the easier mixed methods will be!

Anatomy of Mixed Method Design

By "anatomy," we mean the identification of the main components of the mixed method research project. Briefly, the two main components are the core component (or the "backbone" of the project) and the supplemental project (or the incomplete method, introduced to expand the scope of the project).

The Core Component

The core component of the project is the primary, main, or foundational study in your project. It is the method that is used to address the major part of the research question. Think of the core as the backbone of your project, onto which all other components, methods, or strategies will be attached. The core component is always dominant in mixed method studies. The core method must be conducted at a standard of rigor such that, if all else were to fail, it could be published alone.

The Supplemental Component

Although the core component is always dominant, complete (i.e., scientifically rigorous), and can stand alone, the supplemental component is conducted only to the extent that the researcher obtains the information needed and could not be published alone. We therefore refer to the methodological research tool used to obtain supplementary information as a *strategy*, rather than a *method*. The supplemental project, conducted alongside the core method, is relatively independent but joins the main project at the *point of interface*, or where the two methods come together.

Theoretical Drive

> The theoretical drive is the overall inductive or deductive direction of a research project.

The *theoretical drive* is the conceptual direction of the project overall and is identified from the research question. What is the overall purpose of the research? Is it for exploration? Or is it for theory testing? If it is to explore and to describe some phenomena, the research is working inductively. One may argue that qualitative inquiry involves verification, and therefore is not purely inductive, but the *drive* may be considered the general, overall stance. Note that the theoretical drive guides the use of the core method, so we call a study either qualitatively-driven or quantitatively-driven, denoting the drive in upper-case letters: QUAL for qualitatively-driven and QUAN for quantitatively-driven. The supplemental component is indicated with lower-case letters. Therefore, we record a qualitatively-driven project with a quantitative supplemental component as QUAL-*quan*; conversely, a QUAN-*qual* project is quantitatively-driven, despite the qualitative supplementary project, matching the direction of the core component.

Pacing

> Pacing is the mode of synchronization of the core and the supplemental components.

Pacing refers to the mode in which the core and complementary component are synchronized. There are two main modes of pacing: simultaneous (also labeled "concurrent" [Creswell & Plano Clark, 2007]) and sequential. When conducting a simultaneous mixed method design, both the core and the supplementary components are conducted at the same time, and indicated with a + (plus) sign. When using simultaneous mixed method design, it is important to keep both components separate, so that questions, data, and analysis do not merge. This is of particular risk when conducting QUAL-*qual* sequential mixed method design, when theoretically a researcher may be conducting a secondary analysis using the same data (and perhaps supplementing it with some new data) but focusing on a different dimension of the phenomenon under investigation using one or more strategies drawn from a different method. If a project is paced sequentially, this is indicated with an—>(arrow), so that a qualitatively-driven project with a quantitative supplemental component is labeled as QUAL—>*quan* and QUAN—>*qual* indicates a quantitatively-driven project with a qualitative supplemental component.

Combinations of different core and supplemental components make eight possible mixed method designs. Nomenclature for different types of mixed method designs is presented in Box 2.1.

Box 2.1: Eight types of mixed methods design

QUAL + *quan*:   Qualitative core component of the project (inductive theoretical drive) with a *simultaneous* quantitative supplementary component.

QUAL → *quan*:   Qualitative core component of the project (inductive theoretical drive) with a *sequential* quantitative supplementary component.

QUAL + *qual*:   Qualitative core component of the project (inductive theoretical drive) with a *simultaneous* qualitative supplementary component.

QUAL → *qual*:   Qualitative core component of the project (inductive theoretical drive) with a *sequential* qualitative supplementary component.

QUAN + *qual*:   Quantitative core component of the project (deductive theoretical drive) with a *simultaneous* qualitative supplementary component.

QUAN → *qual*:   Quantitative core component of the project (deductive theoretical drive) with a *sequential* qualitative supplementary component.

QUAN + *quan*:   Quantitative core component of the project (deductive theoretical drive) with a *simultaneous* quantitative supplementary component.

QUAN → *quan*:   Quantitative core component of the project (deductive theoretical drive) with a *sequential* quantitative supplementary component.

An earlier version of Box 2.1 was previously published as Morse, J. M., Wolfe, R., & Niehaus, L. (2006). Principles and procedures for maintaining validity for mixed method design. In Leslie Curry, Renée Shield, & Terrie Wetle (Eds.) *Qualitative Methods in Research and Public Health: Aging and Other Special Populations.* (pp. 66 & 67). Washington, DC: GSA and APHA. Reprinted with permission of the American Public Health Association.

Point of Interface

The *point of interface* is the position in which the core and supplement component meet during the conduct of the research. Usually this is in the *results point of interface*, that is, in the writing of the research results ("research narrative") when findings emanating from the core component form the theoretical base of the results, and the results from the supplemental project embellish and add to the description of

> The *point of interface* is the position in which the two methods join—either in the data analysis or in the narrative of the results.

the core results. In addition to considering the "dominance" of the two components, conceiving how the results will be written up will assist in the determination of which method forms the core component, particularly in QUAL-*qual* projects. For instance, if you are preparing a study using grounded theory and phenomenological interviews, the grounded theory component MUST serve as the core component and MUST form textual the theoretical base of the results. Grounded theory describes process and develops midrange theory. Its scope both in abstraction and over time is more expansive than phenomenology (with results that add depth, but only in "snapshots," as it does not do change and transitions well). Therefore, phenomenological interviews serve as the strategy rather than as the method. We will address this issue further in Chapter 6.

> The core and the supplement strategies meet in two positions: the analytic point of interface and the results point of interface.

The analytic point of interface: The second position where the studies meet is in the analysis where, in a QUAN-*qual* study, the results of the supplementary qualitative component are transformed from textual to numerical data, and incorporated into the quantitative analysis. With this design, the qualitative study must meet certain requirements (see Chapter 8): All participants must have been asked the same questions (preferably in the same order), and these questions are then coded and the responses moved in to the quantitative data set as variables for analysis. The qualitative method that is best suited to such data transformation is semistructured research.

Doing Mixed Method Research

> Principle #3: Recognize and respect the project's theoretical drive.

You must always be consciously aware of the theoretical drive or conceptual direction in which your project is moving overall (i.e., consider: Are you working inductively or deductively?), and this is *determined by the research question*. The theoretical drive guides the main study or *core component* for which the primary method is used. Outlining your design will help you understand this, and we will guide you through how to sketch out the projects and the sequences and how to denote the core component (i.e., the main method—and the theoretical drive) in upper-case letters and supplementary components (or additional strategies) in lower-case letters. Consider the *pacing* of the project—how the two projects will be conducted, *simultaneously* (at the same time, of course), indicated by a (+) sign, or one after the other, or *sequentially*, indicated by an arrow (—>).

Now, think about the question: "Are you working inductively or deductively?" The theoretical drive is usually evident by answering this question. But there are two traps in determining the theoretical drive. First, the order in which the components are actually conducted may not be consistent with the theoretical drive or the pacing of the project. For instance, in a QUAL-*quan* study, the theoretical drive is qualitative, the core method may be grounded theory, and the supplemental strategy used may be a physiological measure of anxiety. When conducting the grounded theory, the interviewer may use retrospective interviews. Meanwhile, the researcher may obtain the anxiety scores for the past 6 months from the participants' counseling records. As the grounded theory is constructed for the past year, the physiological scores are inserted to increase our understanding of the participants' experience. Thus, the chronological order of presentation of each component does *not* necessarily indicate the theoretical drive.

If we have a mixed method design that has a supplemental component from the *same paradigm* as the core component (i.e., you have a *qualitative* core and a *qualitative* supplemental strategy, or a *quantitative* core and a *quantitative* strategy), then conducting the research is relatively easy. You will probably not get into difficulties with the sampling frame or with the way you are thinking about the data (descriptively or testing). Be true to the theoretical drive in your project (i.e., the inductive or deductive direction, as the case may be), in particular when *it comes time to write the narrative of the findings*. The core component provides the theoretical/analytical base from which you write (think of it as the main story), and the supplement component will provide information that will embellish this theoretical base.

> **Principle #4:** Recognize the role of the supplemental component.

Core Component: Conducting the core component part of the project should be easy—you follow standard research rules outlined in many basic research texts.

Supplemental Component: Again, the supplemental component is conducted in a textbook fashion according to the method as dictated by the research question, with some considerations for sampling, the degree to which to project is completed, and how the projects meet at the point of interface.

> **Principle #5:** Adhere to the methodological assumptions of each method.

Problems occur when we have a supplemental component from a different paradigm. The golden rule is that this supplemental component must adhere to its own inductive or deductive principles. The tricky part is fitting it in somehow with the main (core) method for:

> The supplemental component must adhere to its own inductive or deductive principles.

- selecting the sample
- meeting the main study at the point of interface

Between these two points, the supplemental component is conducted as recommended in research texts, except it is completed only to the point that the researcher is certain of the findings and has his or her answer. So,

- *if* it is a qualitative supplemental component, saturation may not be reached;
- *if* it is a quantitative supplemental component, nonparametric statistics may be used, or the measure obtained may be compared with external norms rather than calculated internally on data obtained.

Methodological problems arise when the researcher has two projects each from different paradigm (i.e., working with a qualitative methods and a quantitative supplemental project or vice versa).

If your question is qualitatively-driven, select an appropriate qualitative method and plan for a purposeful and/or theoretical sample,

Qualitatively-
driven = inductive
theoretical drive
Quantitatively-
driven = deductive
theoretical drive

methods of analysis, presentation of the results according to the level of theoretical development, and so forth.

If the main study is quantitatively-driven, abide by all of the assumptions and rules of quantitative inquiry. This includes: the rules of formulating a question or the form of the hypothesis, considerations for instrumentation selection, the rules of sample (appropriateness: randomization [from an appropriate sample] and adequacy [size]), selection of appropriate statistical tests, and so forth.

Principle #6: Carefully consider the pacing of the components.

Remember that the core method used to address the research question in the main study is the "standard method" for whatever method you are using. The core component (main study) is complete and rigorous.

If the qualitative and the quantitative projects are conducted at the same time, this is a *simultaneous mixed method design* and is denoted with a + sign. Simultaneous mixed method designs, and their characteristics, are shown on Table 2.1.

Table 2.1 Types and characteristics of simultaneous mixed method designs

Simultaneous mixed method designs	Characteristics of the design
QUAL + *qual*	This design comprises: • A qualitatively-driven core component • A qualitative supplementary component The core and supplemental components are conducted *simultaneously*.
QUAL + *quan*	This design comprises: • A qualitatively-driven core component • A quantitative supplementary component The core and supplemental components are conducted *simultaneously*.
QUAN + *quan*	This design comprises: • A quantitatively-driven core component • A quantitative supplementary component The core and supplemental components are conducted *simultaneously*.
QUAN + *qual*	This design comprises: • A quantitatively-driven core component • A qualitative supplementary component The core and supplemental components are conducted *simultaneously*.

If the two components are conducted one after the other, with the core component conducted first followed by the supplementary component, we have a *sequential mixed method design, denoted with an arrow* —>. Possible sequential designs, and their characteristics, appear on Table 2.2.

Of course, these notations may be extended as the design becomes more complex. Some of these variations are discussed in Chapter 10.

When the mixed method design involves qualitative and quantitative components, sampling becomes tricky. For example, if a project is quantitatively-driven (i.e., QUAN), a quantitative method is being used as the core (primary) method and a qualitative supplemental strategy is *used to obtain an enhanced description, understanding, or explanation of the phenomenon under investigation*, then the issue is *sampling* and the researcher must ask questions such as: What will we use for the qualitative sample? Should we select participants from the quantitative sample or draw a separate one? It is often the case

> Principle #7: Sampling must be compatible with the assumptions belonging to the method or strategy it serves.

Table 2.2 Sequential mixed method designs and their characteristics

Sequential mixed method designs	Characteristics of the designs
QUAL—>*qual*	This design comprises: • A qualitatively-driven core component • A qualitative supplementary component The core and supplemental components are conducted *sequentially*.
QUAL—>*quan*	This design comprises: • A qualitatively-driven core component • A quantitative supplementary component The core and supplemental components are conducted *sequentially*.
QUAN—>*quan*	This design comprises: • A quantitatively-driven core component • A quantitative supplementary component The core and supplemental components are conducted *sequentially*.
QUAN—>*qual*	This design comprises: • A quantitatively-driven core component • A qualitative supplementary component The core and supplemental components are conducted *sequentially*.

Table 2.3 Core positions of the point of interface

Point of interface	Description
Analytical point of interface	• The supplemental component fits into the core component in the analysis of the core data.
	• For instance, with a QUAN + *qual* design, *if* the qualitative component meets certain assumptions, data collected by using the *qual* supplemental strategy may be transformed numerically and incorporated into the QUAN data set of the core component as additional variable(s) and analyzed quantitatively.
	• This integration of data has to be done just before the core data are analyzed.
Results point of interface	• The supplemental component fits into the core component in the results narrative of the core component.
	• Data from the supplemental component are analyzed separately from the core data, and the *results* from the supplemental strategy are incorporated into the findings of the core narrative, informing the findings of the core method.
	• The findings are always written so that the core project results form the theoretical base of the study, and the supplementary findings embellish, detail, and supplement the narrative.

that one sample cannot be adopted *carte blanche* into the supplemental component, so possible alternatives for sampling must be considered.

The position where the supplemental component fits into the core component usually occurs in one of two places: in the analysis of the core data (i.e., the analytic core) or in the results narrative of the core component (see Table 2.3). The conditions necessary for the integration of each supplementary component to the core component and the procedures will be described later (see Chapters 8 and 9).

Examples of Mixed Method Designs

In this section, we discuss examples of various types of mixed method designs, considering the role of the supplemental component (Table 2.4).

Note that each component contributes to the scientific contribution of the project—that is, is directly relevant to answering the research questions. Sometimes a researcher will have to "detour"—conduct a small qualitative project to assist with the *mechanics* of the project (perhaps to determine why refusal to participate is too high and to

Table 2.4 Role of the supplemental component for the major designs

Mixed method designs	Supplemental component	Role of the supplemental component
QUAL +/—>*qual*	*qual*	• Elicit another perspective or dimension • Obtain data that the first method cannot access
QUAL +/—>*quan*	*quan*	• Enhance description (how much many, high, fast, loud, etc.) • Enable the testing of an emerging conjecture
QUAN +/—>*qual*	*qual*	• Provide explanation • Obtain description that the first method cannot access
QUAN +/—>*quan*	*quan*	• Add a second layer of description • Provide supplemental evidence

increase enrollment [Donavan et al., 2002]). Because this detour does not contribute directly to the research question, it does not play a role in the mixed methods project per se. Such projects are incidental to the research, not a part of the design (unless, in this case, your topic is enrollment), and are therefore not, as the authors and Creswell and Plano Clark (2007) have classified, "embedded" in the study.

QUAN + *qual* Design

This is a simultaneous quantitatively-driven mixed method design, with the point of interface in the analytic core. The core component is measurement or even experimental method design; the supplemental strategy is to provide explanation or to obtain description that the first method cannot access.

An example of such a study may be a survey with 10% of the items written as semistructured open-ended questions to address the quantitative component. The research question was "What are the incidence and severity of untoward effects to participants of unstructured interviews?" Given the wealth of research literature that refers to the use of unstructured interviews and researchers' awareness of potential harm arising from these interviews, the theoretical drive or overall direction of the inquiry is deductive and quantitative.

The sample size of 517 respondents was large for the management of the textual data, yet the transposition of these qualitative data to enable their incorporation into the statistical analysis was not prohibitive, and the inductive qualitative component greatly added to the validity of the overall project and enhanced description, under-standing, or explanation of the phenomenon under investigation. For instance, qualitative data were obtained about why some research topics could be labeled as emotionally sensitive topics.

Six response categories for this variable emerged from the data. These data revealed that during interviews, participants recalled feel-ings about "self issues," "controversial issues," "illness and/or caregiv-ing issues," "mental health issues," "marital and/or parenting issues." For coding all textual responses, it was also necessary to include the following response categories: "Other issues," "More than one of the above," "Not applicable/Difficult to tell/Don't know." A numerical code was then assigned to each response category and this variable was included in the code book for coding of the responses. However, the qualitative responses were also analyzed qualitatively. The loss of detail that occurs with quantitative transposition is costly but must be considered a different type of information provided.

QUAN—>*qual* Design

This is a quantitatively-driven, sequential, mixed method design. An example of such a study may be a quantitative survey of a neighbor-hood. Analysis revealed no correlation between working mothers of toddlers and the use of day care facilities. Follow-up qualitative inter-views were then conducted with a sample of "good informants" from the QUAN sample. The supplemental qualitative data revealed that many of the fathers in these areas were students with flexible sched-ules; they organized their schedules to assume care of their children during the day and elected to do their studies in the hours their wives were able to be home. This flexible arrangement for child care had not been anticipated by the researchers, and the subsequent qualitative component was necessary to provide explanation for the unexpected findings.

QUAL + *quan* Design

This study is qualitatively-driven, with a simultaneous, quantitative supplementary component.

An example of this design may be a study exploring the mutual consolation that occurs between relatives of critically ill patients in the family waiting room. The researcher may observe that the mothers of these patients go forward to the head of the bed, while fathers stay back at the foot of the bed. If we could objectively meas-ure the distance between these parents, the description would be more compelling.

The researcher realized that a "rough" measure of the distances between the parents could be unobtrusively measured by counting the number of floor tiles between them. In this way, the results contrib-uted to the description of the need for mutual consolation between the relatives.

QUAL—>*quan* Design

This is a qualitatively-driven design with a quantitative sequential supplemental component using a *data collection strategy*.

An example of this study would be to explore the mutual consolation that occurs between relatives of critically ill patients in the family waiting room. The researcher may observe that the relatives are anxious and wish to describe the degree of anxiety manifest by using a standardized anxiety scale (a supplemental data collection strategy). In this way, the scores were obtained separately from the relatives and compared with external norms. The results were added to the description of the need for mutual consolation between the relatives.

QUAL—>*quan* design

This example is the same design as above, with the exception of *using a supplementary data analysis* strategy.

In our example of relatives waiting, we may observe that those who appear to meditate have less need for the support provided by relatives. In interviews with these relatives, those who are spiritual have spoken of their use of meditation. This information may be quantified by rigorously transforming and coding the data and then conducting nonparametric statistical analyses on the results to determine whether there are significant associations between relevant variables. Note that this data analysis strategy is sequential, because the transformation of the qualitative data cannot be performed until the qualitative analysis is completed and these results inform the research findings rather than building the findings per se.

Sampling Issues for Mixed Methods Design

When the mixed method design involves qualitative and quantitative components, sampling becomes tricky. With a quantitatively-driven, qualitative supplemental design (QUAN-*qual*), the researcher must consider:

- the quantitative sample is too large for qualitative use (with the exception of qualitative semistructured interview as a method); and
- the quantitative sample has been randomly selected. With the small size of the qualitative sample:
  - If the researcher samples (perhaps randomly) from this sample, it is possible that the qualitative interviews will have very poor and possibly no information that will answer the research question.
  - If the qualitative researcher uses all the quantitative sample, unless she or he is using semistructured interviews, she or he will drown in data. If the studies are conducted sequentially,

it is possible that the sample cannot be located, and not available, anyway.

Conversely, with a qualitatively-driven, quantitative supplemental design (QUAL-*quan*):

- the qualitative sample is too small for quantitative use (with the exception of small sample non-parametric analysis), and,
- the qualitative sample has been purposefully selected and from a quantitative perspective, is biased.
  - If the quantitative researcher uses this sample, it is possible that the quantitative analysis will be meaningless.
  - If the quantitative researcher measures some dimension in qualitative sample (using it also as the supplementary sample) the results will be useless UNLESS she or he compares these results with norms obtained elsewhere (these are often available with the instrument). As with quantitatively-driven projects, if the studies are conducted sequentially, it is possible that the sample cannot be located, and not available, anyway.

Therefore, where will the quantitative researcher obtain his or her sample?

We will discuss this question of sampling in greater detail later. Meanwhile, think about the problem.

Pitfalls with Mixed Method Design

Although mixed method designs strengthen research by making it more comprehensive, it is not always easy to do. Some common errors make it tricky and may threaten the validity of the entire project:

1. *Ignoring the theoretical drive or being unaware of the theoretical drive*

   Can one have a core and a supplementary component of equal theoretical "weight"—a parallel design, so to speak? Some authors write of *equivalent designs* (Creswell & Plano Clark, 2007). However, if projects have equal weight, what does an "equal weight research question" look like? Are both complete and scientifically rigorous? (If so, one is actually, by definition, conducting multiple method research). How do you write up the findings of these studies—two projects cannot jointly form a theoretical base! Ask yourself, are these two components really representative of around the same phenomenon?

2. *Failure to recognize or respect the core component*

   The core component is the theoretical "base" of the project, which the findings of the supplemental project usually fit into. Failure to recognize which component is the theoretical foundation makes it much more difficult to "write up" the findings as a coherent port on the study. Ignoring which component is the core may also result in sloppy practices when collecting data, and later we will discuss why the core and the supplemental components must be conducted separately.

3. *Ignoring the methodological assumptions of the supplementary method*

   Every research method has its particular quirks that must be respected and followed. If you do not have these assumptions clearly demarcated, it is possible that important assumptions will be overlooked and ignored. For instance, if you have a QUAL-*quan* design, later, in Chapter 6 we will discuss how to overcome the limitations of the qualitative purposeful sample when conducting the quantitative supplementary component; or, alternatively, how you select a qualitative sample when conducting a quantitatively-driven project with a qualitative supplementary component. Further, if one is conducting a QUAN + *qual* project and wishes to incorporate the qualitative data into the quantitative data set for analysis, thereby making the supplementary method fit the requirements the core method, techniques of data transformation are essential, and the qualitative data must have a certain form for such transformation to be possible (see Chapter 9).

4. *Not conducting an armchair walkthrough*

   Conducting an armchair walkthrough is deliberately envisioning your project and the alternative designs and all possible outcomes. It is imagining your project step by step, to foresee problems and the advantages and disadvantages of conducting your project using all available alternatives. It enables you, to the best of your ability, to select the design wisely.

   Using the armchair walkthrough, smart researchers are able to think through their project to the end result, anticipate the sample needs for each study, the type of data that will be obtained, the methods used and why, how the core and the supplemental components will interface, and what the results will look like. You will be able to see how they will fit at the point of interface, and what your end product will look like. Now—diagram it!

   Such smart conceptualizing, putting yourself several steps ahead of the project, while, at the same time, planning (or even working with the data if a supplementary project is going to emerge), is crucial. We spoke of the difficulties of having a grounded theory study in a QUAN-qual design: If you needed the grounded theory, perhaps you should have been doing a single-method qualitatively-driven project or should move to a multiple-method project. The lack of theoretical fit between some methods is insurmountable—not only do some methods not fit, they do not make conceptual/theoretical sense either. Mull this over—we will return to it later.

Reading the Flowcharts

Examples of flow charts illustrating types of mixed method designs are included in each chapter describing each particular method (Chapters 8 and 9). Developing flowcharts for each mixed method design allows us explore both the core and the supplementary component clearly, illustrate the pacing, and show where these components meet (interface). Note that the *point of interface* is usually in the core narrative

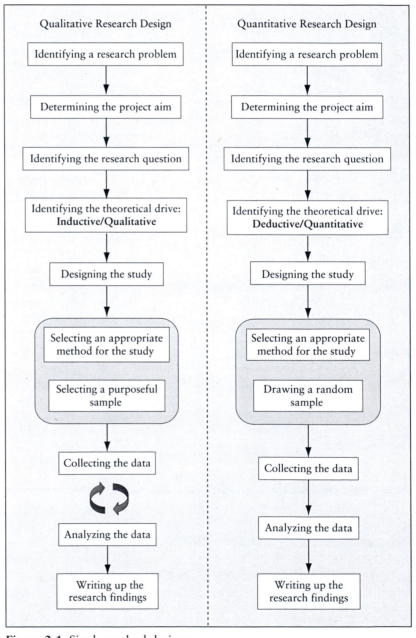

Figure 2.1 Single method designs

of the results section or, less commonly, in the core data analysis section. Separating each component by providing each with its own pathway in the flowchart helps us manage each data set, understand how they are paced (sequentially or simultaneously), and to note quickly the intricacies of design that needs to be developed (sample/participants, instruments/interviews or observations, and so forth). Of greater importance, the flowcharts are a constant reminder of the theoretical drive—to be constantly aware if you are working inductively or deductively.

When you come to a flowchart, read it from the top down and you will notice that it is simply the basic research process. For instance, both qualitative and quantitative research projects start with aims and from the aims a research question develops. Next, choose the method that optimally fits the research question. Then select the setting, choose the sample that best answers the question and fits the method, and collect your data. The analysis follows and the results are presented. When presenting a mixed method, we place the core project in the left-hand pathway and the supplemental component in the right.

In Figure 2.1, we illustrate the basic research process using two flow charts to show you how easy they are to read from the top down. We have outlined a quantitative project in the left diagram and qualitative project in the right in Figure 2.1. These are the flowcharts for your basic quantitative and qualitative project, from identifying the research problem, as normally conducted.

3

Theoretical Drive

Every research project is a process of "finding something out." If the process is one of finding something out when there is little in the library on a topic, you must start from the beginning. You begin without presumptions or a theoretical frame that dictates what variables should be examined or the relationship between these variables. We call this mode of proceeding *induction*. If the study is being conducted for the purpose of testing hypotheses, confirming conjectures, or for testing a theory, the process is called *deduction*. A third mode of thinking inquiry is to move back and forward between induction and deduction throughout the research by first developing conjectures and then systematically testing these conjectures—a process labeled *abduction*.

> Principle #3: Recognize and respect the project's theoretical drive.

Doing a research project always takes researchers to a different stage of understanding in their research program than where they were at the beginning; it never leaves researchers at the same level of knowledge that they had before they started. Even if the hypotheses are not supported, knowing when something is *not* significant is important and something to be gained in a research program.

The induction/deductive direction of the research project is labeled as the *theoretical drive* (Morse, 1991, 2003; Morse et al., 2006), and refers to whether the conceptual process in the study is one of discovery or confirming. When the project is a single-method design, the theoretical drive is usually easy to identify. Qualitative inquiry usually (but not always) uses inductive methods, and deductive, or theory testing, research—again usually, but not always—uses quantitative methods. Exceptions to this are possible when, for instance in a quantitative project, the phenomena can't be measured, qualitative data may be used in a quantitative design, or when, in a discovery design, quantitative data are used as a "fishing-trip," and techniques of exploratory data analysis (Tukey, 1977) are used. Abduction is used in grounded theory and sometimes in ethnography, and in the interview process "checking" within and between participants when attaining validity in the development of a qualitative study (see Meadows & Morse, 2001). However, abduction generally moves in inductive mode overall, working in a stepwise fashion, but more slowly and deliberately than in an inductive mode, so for our purposes we classify it as induction.

In all research, the project has an *aim* and from this we can identify the inductive/deductive direction of the project's theoretical drive. There is always a "match" between the theoretical drive and the core component. The main project with a qualitative theoretical drive MUST use a qualitative method, and with a quantitative theoretical drive must use a quantitative method.

The research questions, derived from the aim, will usually dictate the other components of the study, which may be qualitative or quantitative, and paced sequentially or simultaneously, regardless of the overall drive. This means that a QUAN mixed method project with a *qual* supplemental component will be conducted deductively, BUT the *qual* component, between the sample and its analysis, will be conducted *inductively*, according to the rules of qualitative inquiry. These results are then moved into the quantitative findings and the results point of interface.

Conversely, if it is a QUAL-*quan* mixed method design, the quantitative supplemental component (*quan*) from sample to analysis is *conducted deductively according to the principles of quantitative inquiry*, and these results are moved into the qualitative findings at the results point of interface.

How do you know whether the theoretical drive is inductive and qualitative or deductive and quantitative? It should be evident from the aims: Do the aims demand exploration or description of testing? Aims that are inductive are generally descriptive or exploratory; deductive questions are generally better developed with formal hypotheses or with the framework/theory evident.

How do you know what strategies to use for the supplemental component?

The research questions emerge from the *aims* (although some researchers replace research questions with sub-aims). Research questions dictate the type of strategies that will provide the *best* answers and sometimes even the pacing of these components.

But we are a little ahead of ourselves—let us first address the complexity of mixed methods studies.

When Are Mixed Method Studies Used?

Mixed method studies are usually used in three circumstances:

1. *If the question does not completely encompass the phenomena*: In this case, a supplemental arm may be added to the study and be described as a part of the proposal.

   If it is clear that whatever is unknown may be incorporated into the study by adding another method, then the supplementary component is planned and added to the proposal at that time.

> The components of the study are dictated by the research questions.

> A QUAN core component will be conducted deductively, but the *qual* supplemental component, inductively.

> A QUAL core component will be conducted inductively, but the *quan* supplemental component, deductively.

2. *If, during the course of the inquiry, interesting or unexpected phenomena are revealed*: In this case, the investigator may recognize that these new phenomena could be incorporated into the study while the present one is ongoing, plan the supplementary component (and obtain permission from the change in protocol from the institutional review board), and conduct the supplementary component simultaneously. This occasion usually occurs only in qualitatively-driven studies, and of course would be a QUAL + *quan* or QUAL + *qual* design.

3. *Unexpected findings are revealed in a quantitatively-driven study*: Following the analysis of quantitative study, the researchers may be puzzled by unexpected findings. They may then decide to conduct a small qualitative study to account for these and to include in the results (this design would then be a QUAN—>*qual*).

Emergent Mixed Method Studies

Although the first design, planned at the proposal stage, may be either sequentially or simultaneously conducted, the supplemental components added in circumstance (2) to (3) above during the course of the project are called *emergent designs*.

It is not possible to have a project without a theoretical drive. Research always goes somewhere; it never stands still theoretically. Because of this, in mixed method design the core component of the project is always reflects the theoretical drive and the data or findings of the supplementary component fit into the core component. We disagree with "equivalent design" as proposed by Morgan (1998) and Creswell (Creswell et al., 2003). Although Morgan's priority-sequence model (1998) includes principal (QUAL or QUAN) and complementary (*qual* or *quan*) methods, it does not recognize the theoretical drive that dictates the direction (inductive or deductive) of the research. Similarly, the "nested design" (Creswell et al., 2003) provides for equal dominance of the components of the project, suggesting that the components can be merged—something that is not possible, as one component must always fit into the other (Morse et al., 2006).

Remember: The major difficulties in conducting mixed method research and the greatest threats to validity occur in mixed method designs when the two methodological components are drawn from different paradigms: that is, when qualitative and quantitative methodological strategies are used in the same mixed method study.

The Role of Theoretical Drive in Mixed Method Research

Research is purposeful. The nature and type of the research question dictates the overall purpose, design, types of data sources, sampling and recruitment strategies, data collection options, approaches to analysis and interpretation, and types of results eventually obtained. Considering how to conduct the research extends from the research question (Richards & Morse, 2007), which forces the researcher to identify the study as using an inductive or deductive theoretical drive and to select an appropriate design. Consider: Is the purpose of the research to learn about a particular problem? Understand a situation? Assess the effect of an intervention? Test a theory?

We usually associate induction with qualitative methods and deduction with quantitative methods. In general terms, the process of induction can be seen as a process of finding out what "is" or seeking meaning, whereas the process of deduction can be seen as a process of testing or, for experimental design, of finding out what "is not" by the testing of theoretical propositions.

> Induction is moving from the empirical world to more abstract concepts and theory.

Induction is usually characterized as the process of understanding, eliciting meaning, or building theory by moving from empirical or "real world" situations or contexts to generalizations in the form of abstract concepts, theories, and/or hypotheses. Data are *made* and analyzed in keeping with the underlying philosophical assumptions of the particular research question and method. Most important, however, are the ways to look and think. Induction involves deriving generalizations from the data without the imposition of a priori assumptions and/or preconceived theoretical notions. The researcher's ability to adopt new ways of seeing, maintain an orientation of discovery, and derive the question(s) from the data are central to induction. These abilities require an analytical stance including flexibility, patience, time and, most importantly, an orientation to understanding puzzling phenomena, seeking meaning, making sense. It is not about technique; rather, it is a way of thinking (Richards & Morse, 2007).

> Deduction is moving from theories and hypotheses by testing, working from the general to the particular.

Conversely, deduction is characterized as the process of testing or refuting theories or hypotheses by moving from the general to the particular or "real" world. Deduction is motivated by a priori assumptions or theoretical propositions. It is an approach to data analysis, explanation, and theory building in which conjectural hypotheses (predictions) can be tested and for which no negative cases then are found (Miller & Brewer, 2003) or as probabilities. The researcher translates the assumptions or theoretical propositions into quantifiable forms of instruments (or locates suitable instruments), pilot tests them, and ensures reliability and validity (unless using established validated instruments) to which everyone in the relevant population is expected to be able respond equally well. Data are sought that are specific to the purpose of testing and refuting already developed concepts.

Exceptions to this rule occur when quantitative methods are used, albeit less than ideally, for inductive purposes and sometimes when qualitative inquiry is used for deductive purposes. For instance, statistical surveys may be used in projects with an inductive drive, and qualitative strategies are used in projects with a deductive drive, as is frequently the case in evaluation research. Evaluation is usually oriented to looking for evidence of predetermined desired outcomes as most interventions are funded on the basis of what they propose to accomplish. Good evaluation also usually allows for discovering "unintended consequences," particularly in demonstration or development stages. Thus, like other research, comprehensive evaluations may have both inductive and deductive phases within an overriding theoretical drive.

An example of a quantitative project with an inductive theoretical drive may be a "fishing trip" (i.e., when a large amount of quantitative data "mined" by the researchers, exploratory, looking for significant relationships [Tukey, 1977]). Some researchers have engaged in an entire inductive program of research (with the overall purpose of model development) made up of a series of individual deductive projects. For instance, the development of Leventhal's health belief model is a particularly interesting example of a research program with an inductive theoretical thrust made up entirely of quantitative hypothesis-testing projects. Experience was seen as "getting in the way"; after 20 years of research, Leventhal identified the need for qualitative narratives, and the conclusion was that the narratives and scales did not match up (Leventhal, 1993).

Conversely, a quantitative project with a deductive theoretical drive may use qualitative data; this occurs when the phenomena are not measurable or a project with the application of an a priori theoretical framework to qualitative data to "prove" the researcher's agenda. Another exception is a qualitative project such as applying scaffolds and skeletons (Morse & Mitcham, 2002) deductively, or with the use of abduction, as mentioned previously.

It is important that the researcher recognize and be explicit about the starting point for the research: that is, whether it is exploring the unknown or building on what is already known. Thus, knowledge is advanced.

Note that when the supplemental component is from the opposite paradigm (i.e., a quantitative supplemental project with a qualitative core or vice versa), the shift between the inductive and deductive components of research does *not* alter the overall theoretical drive of the project, although the supplemental component is conceptually and analytically "moving" in the opposite direction. The overall theoretical drive *always dictates* the method used in the core, or the main component, and indicated by upper-case letters, regardless of the strategies used in the supplemental component.

Absence of conscious attention to theoretical drive often results in serious threats to validity. Researchers lose their awareness of the core focus and direction of mixed method research, resulting in errors in design, analysis, or the reporting of findings; the research risks lacking methodological coherence, so that the validity of the project may be compromised.

> The theoretical drive always dictates the core method used for conducting the core component of the project.

Ramifications of Paradigmatic Assumptions in Mixed Method Research

As noted previously, inductive qualitative methods and deductive quantitative methods have incompatible components in the research process: For instance, a sample cannot be both random and purposeful and qualitative data cannot be added.

Sampling Problems

If conducting mixed method research with a qualitative and a quantitative method, sampling becomes an immediate issue; this will be discussed in Chapter 6. Basically, the difficulty is when the two components are from a different research paradigm, and the sample used by the core component is not appropriate to use for the supplementary component. If the core component is a large quantitatively-driven study, then a qualitative purposive sample may be drawn from that sample according to the principles of qualitative sampling or a separate qualitative sample is drawn. If the core method is qualitatively-driven the qualitative sample is too small, and has not been obtained by processes of randomization. Again, a separate quantitative sample may be drawn, or, if the purpose of the quantification is to add to the descriptions of the sample, comparison of the quantitative scores may be made by using the external norms that are obtained by other developers of the instrument or from the literature.

Problems in the Use of Theoretical Drive

Not Recognizing the Conceptual Contribution to the Project

Determining the theoretical drive is not a democratic process. By this we mean that the theoretical drive is not decided by the size (N) of the sample or the extensiveness of the project, *but by the theoretical contribution of the project*. For example, if a researcher conducts some focus groups and then develops a survey from these focus groups, this is NOT a *qual*—>QUAN design! Because the survey is developed from the focus groups, and the design of the survey is depended on the focus group data, the study is QUAL, or a qualitatively-driven QUAL—>*quan* design.

Disregarding the Theoretical Drive

Disregarding the theoretical drive of a project (or the theoretical thrust of a research program) involving both qualitative and quantitative methods leaves the fit of the components loose and the pacing of project components (or projects) unspecified, nonspecific, and/or disconnected. Further, mixed method research involving both qualitative and quantitative methods poses particular challenges because of the shifting assumptions in moving between the inductive and deductive theoretical drives. Absence of conscious attention to theoretical drive often results in serious threats to validity. Researchers lose their awareness of the core focus and direction of mixed method research, resulting in errors in design, analysis, or the reporting of findings. The research risks lacking methodological coherence such that the validity of the project may be compromised (Morse, Niehaus, & Wolfe, 2005).

What about Equivalent Designs?

An important principle of mixed methods designs is that the supplementary project must always fit into the core component. If the two methods are to be integrated (i.e., at the point of interface) in the presentation of the results, the findings of the *core component provides the theoretical foundation of this narrative*. That is, the findings of the core component, driven by the overall theoretical drive, are the base (or structure) into which the supplementary findings must fit. Your writing will not make very much sense and will be difficult to conduct if you are treating each component as equal. We will return to this point in several sections of the book, explaining why, even if the project is QUAL + *qual*, certain qualitative methods used MUST be dominant and form the theoretical foundation of the study. If the results are QUAN + *quan*, the same restrictions apply with the findings narrative.

4

Pacing the Components

Pacing, the synchronization of the core component and the supplementary component, is crucial to the conduct of mixed method design. At the most obvious level, both components may be conducted *simultaneously* (sometimes also called "concurrently" [Creswell & Plano Clark, 2007; Morgan, 1998]), or sequentially (one after the other). The pacing of these components has important implications for the mode of interaction of the two components, for sampling, and for the point of interface.

Pacing is the synchronization of the core component and the supplementary component.

Simultaneous Mixed Method Design (+)

Simultaneous mixed method design, indicated with a + (plus) sign, is usually planned (but not always) at the proposal phase of the project. During the project's design phase, the researcher may recognize the limitations of the core component and be aware of the gaps or what will *not* be known if the core method is used alone. At that time, the researcher may decide to compensate for the perceived inadequacy by planning an additional supplementary component. This supplementary component may be conducted either simultaneously with the core component, or sequentially after the completion of the core component.

If, however, during the conduct of a project, the researcher becomes aware that parts of the project are inadequate, and recognizes that additional information would be advantageous, he or she may wish to add a supplementary component to collect this information that would make the project more comprehensive or complete. In this *emergent* design, the supplement component may be added simultaneously or on the completion of the data analysis of the core component (i.e., sequentially), but prior to the writing of the results of the core component.

If the researcher makes arrangements to add the supplementary component simultaneously, while the core component is still being conducted, such changes are dependent on permissions and resources. There are advantages to conducting it simultaneously—mainly that the project is completed more quickly. But there are also disadvantages: If the supplementary project is conceived and conducted after the core component has started, then because data have already been collected from some (but not all) of the participants, the supplementary component's *point of interface*, or where the two methods meet, will always be in the *results narrative*.

Sequential Mixed Method Design (—>)

In sequential mixed method design, the core component is completed before the supplemental component is initiated, and this type of pacing is indicated with an arrow (—>). Sequential mixed method may be planned at the proposal stage or during or after the completion of the core component. Again, the point of interface will always be in the writing of the *results narrative*.

Important things to remember about *pacing* are that it may be (1) planned (designed at the proposal stage) versus (2) unplanned (emergent design) with the need the supplemental component recognized only after the study has commenced. We will next discuss planning the a priori supplemental component versus planning in the midst of the project and "designing on the run."

The Supplemental Component: Designing at the Proposal Stage

Recall that in mixed method design each component, both the core and the supplementary components, are separate, planned, and coordinated. Doing mixed method research is not a haphazard endeavor or something conducted impulsively. If, at the design stage of the study, the researcher can foresee the gaps and the inadequacies that will occur in the completed study because the core method is not comprehensive for the research questions, the researcher may then, at the proposal stage, design a supplemental component to make the project comprehensive. The proposal may be designed to conduct the two components simultaneously or sequentially, with plans for sampling data collection, and to interface the two data sets either in the analysis or to merge in the findings (see Chapter 7). Both methods should be described in the ethics application and budgeted accordingly.

As each component is designed, plans for the incorporation of the data that will be obtained must also be anticipated. It is not just the sample or the data collection that is *paced*, but the entire supplementary component and the *point of interface* of the data or findings must be determined. Finally, the researcher must be able to anticipate how the supplementary component will enhance the project as a whole and make an argument for its inclusion.

Simultaneously Paced Components Designed at the Proposal Stage

Qualitatively-Driven (QUAL) Studies

QUAL + *quan*

When planning a QUAL study exploring perhaps the role of spousal care giving when one spouse is dying at home, the researcher may recognize that the nature of care provided by the care-giving spouse varies by the level of illness.

Gender of the care giver may be easily quantified and comparison of the care giving provided by male and female caregivers will "split" the sample. "Level of illness" may be more difficulty to quantify, but distinct stages in the patient's decline may be identified by level of activity and evidence of disease, as described in the Palliative Performance Scale (Anderson, Downing, & Hill, 1996). The caregiving actions of the spouse within these periods may then be compared and contrasted.

QUAL—>*quan*

The above study may be designed as a QUAL study with a sequential quantitative supplemental component. Suppose a researcher conducted a study of dying at home, exploring one spouse caring for the other. At the end of the study, you recognize that the amount of support given the care giver from others probably dramatically affected their experience. You find a "perceived support" scale. Unfortunately, you can no longer access the original sample, so you draw another sample of spousal caregivers. You rate their care-giving activities, level of illness of spouse, and perceived support.

Quantitatively-Driven (QUAN) Studies

Consider a project that is quantitatively-driven (QUAN), and measurement consists of a quantitative survey. During the design of the project, the researcher recognizes that further clarification of certain survey items is necessary. To do this, the researcher writes open-ended questions into the survey that ask: "Tell me why you selected the above option."

Writing such an open-ended semistructured question elicits the rationale for the previous quantitative selection. Thus, the notation for this design is QUAN + *qual*—a quantitatively-driven study with a quantitative core component and a qualitative simultaneous supplementary component. At the design stage, the researcher must describe in the proposal how she or he intends to analyze the qualitative data: She or he might: (1) Transpose the qualitative data to numerical data and incorporate the responses into the quantitative data set (see Chapter 9); or perhaps (2) keep the qualitative data as qualitative data, perhaps performing some type of content analysis on these data and incorporating insights into the results narrative.

Adding a Supplemental Component: "Designing on the Run"

Because of the emergent nature of research itself—particularly in qualitatively-driven research—the need for a simultaneous supplementary component may not have been anticipated when the project began. After the researcher begins data collection and analysis, important issues may arise that reveal dimensions of the research question that are not addressed using only the proposed research method. When this occurs, the researcher must decide whether:

- to live with the problem or deficiency, perhaps addressing it in the limitations of the study and plan to conduct a subsequent project sometime in the future, *or*
- to redesign the study, adding a mixed method supplementary component, expand the study, and incorporate the additional area in the present study.

Thus, single method projects may develop into a mixed method project after the project start date and ethics approval. This may have the following ramifications for the budget:

- additional financial resources for the supplemental component may not be available, hence the supplemental component may not be possible;
- the researcher may go back to the funding agency and request a funding supplement, so the supplemental component is a possibility;
- the researcher may decide to increase effort (work harder) to incorporate the minor change, so that the supplemental component is conducted, or
- the researcher may decide the additional resources will not have a very great impact on the budget and go ahead with the additional component.

At this time, the researcher must design the *pacing* of the supplemental component with the core component. This includes developing a sampling plan, data collection and analysis, the point of interface of the two data sets, or consideration about how the findings will be incorporated. One final reminder: If you are a student, do not forget to advise your committee of the changes, and do not forget to file a change with your university's institutional review board.

Simultaneously Paced Components Designed After Commencement of the Project

As noted, the pacing of the simultaneous projects is not always planned at the proposal stage and may be initiated during the collection of data for the core project, during a quantitatively- or qualitatively-driven project. Again, the pacing of the two projects and all of the components of the supplemental project must be planned before the supplemental project is implemented. Any necessary approvals must be obtained and any changes to the consent forms made. The host site must be notified as well as the funding agency. The researcher must be clear about the nature of the supplemental project and must plan how the sample will be located, what the nature of the supplemental methods will be, and how the supplemental data will interface with the data from the core component or how the findings will be incorporated with the findings from the core project.

Examples of Simultaneous (+) Pacing

During a qualitatively-driven project (QUAL + *quan*) in the classroom, to investigate how students cheat on examinations, the investigator decided to conduct the study using participant observation. However, in the course of data collection, he decided to incorporate the students' past test scores as an indicator of past performance, possibly with the aid of cheating. The researcher wanted to determine if there are any discrepancies or large swings in scores from the past few weeks when compared with the present test. He suspected that a sudden decrease in exam scores after the clamp-down on cheating may be indicative of past cheating. In this case, the quantitative data become only a small part of the qualitative data set, adding to information about characteristics of each participant.

Sequentially Paced Components Designed at the Proposal Stage

Sequential pacing may be considered relatively clumsy because the core component probably has been completed before the supplementary component is commenced. Sequential pacing is common because, following analysis, the investigators realized there were additional questions that should be answered prior to publication or there would be a serious gap in their study. Without the supplemental study, the core project loses some of its significance. The results of both components are dependent on each other. The design is therefore conceived and added "mid-project."

What Is *Not* a Sequential Mixed Method Design

Losing Your Drive

All of the above sounds very organized and logical—it is. But occasionally, one finds a design that, although it maintains logic and keeps order, is assembled or paced at the end of data collection. This design is an exception: Pacing may become clear only once the pieces of the study are analytically assembled.

For example, in a longitudinal study, the researcher may collect physiological variables at baseline, 3, 6, and 9 months. These measurements are the supplemental components. At that point—9 months—he or she may conduct retrospective grounded theory interviews. Once the grounded theory analysis is completed and the 9-month process has been clarified, using that grounded theory as the base, then place the physiological variables onto this base as interpretative data. What design is this? Yes—QUAL + *quan*. Even though the timing of data collection was "out of sync," once the project is assembled and the pieces placed in temporal order, the pacing and the design of the study becomes clear. This design exemplifies an important point about pacing: *Pacing is* not *a chronological concept, but based on the theoretical needs of the study.*

Exceptions and Other Problems

Ethnography: Simultaneous Mixed Method?

Many investigators employ the ethnographic method and argue that they are conducting mixed methods. However, ethnographic research, by definition, uses participant observation, various types of interviews, field notes, and other strategies. This triad of strategies (plus other data collection strategies if necessary), integrated with the assumptions associated with culture, are what give ethnography its character. It may make your study appealing to a funding agency to describe it as mixed method, but, on the other hand, you may draw a traditional reviewer who disagrees and believes that ethnography does not need to be labeled as such. Where do we fall in this debate? Some of the best examples that illustrate mixed method design are ethnographic studies. Not every study can be neatly classified, and perhaps we should just wait to see what consensus develops.

Testing Qualitative Theory?

A quantitative study that is conducted following a qualitative study in order to confirm the qualitatively derived theory should *not* be a sequential mixed method design. Because each component must be conducted rigorously and stand alone, these projects are usually classified as multiple method design.

*qual—>*QUAN?

Always consider the *purpose* or the role of the components.

Scenerio #1: Conducting a few interviews or focus groups before a quantitative study and using these qualitative interviews to develop items for questionnaire, is *not* a *qual—>*QUAN mixed method study. In this case, the qualitative interviews are a methodological strategy to develop the quantitative instrument, rather than the component of the study that contributes to the theoretical framework or that contributes a separate set of findings to the study.

Scenerio #2: A "few" focus groups conducted prior to a survey is not a *qual—>*QUAN design, but a QUAL—>*quan* design. Always consider the purpose of each component. The framework of the study and the text for survey items was derived from the focus groups. In other words, the framework of the entire study is resting conceptually on the focus groups—indicating an inductive drive! This means that one must look at the contributions of each method, and the theoretical drive is more significant than the pacing—which can be considered an organizational structure.

The Supplementary Afterthought

On completing a quantitative study, the researcher may obtain unexpected results, and a qualitative study may then be conducted to explain these results. For instance, the investigator may conduct a survey of the community with surprising findings and then conduct ethnographic fieldwork, seeking the reason for these unexpected results in the survey. In this case, the pacing of the supplementary project is really an afterthought, but still a QUAN—>*qual* mixed method design.

Remember: When conducting mixed method design, the researcher does not "blend" data collection methods but keeps data from each component separate until the point of analytic or theoretical interface. Pacing is a thoughtful and deliberate endeavor in which the researcher is acutely aware of working either inductively or deductively, of all the pertinent qualitative and quantitative methodological assumptions— and of meeting these assumptions—and of the necessary strategies to maintain rigor at the point of interface.

5

The Point of Interface

Mixed method design is systematic. At best, researchers conduct two components, keeping each data set separate until the *point of interface*, or the position in the research process in which the two components meet. These two data sets do not mingle nor blend—each is handled appropriately according to its modus operandi until the researcher intentionally brings the two operations together, at a time when both of the two methods are "ready" to be combined. In mixed method design, the point of interface can occur only in two positions:

1. *in the analysis of the core component.* The core and the supplemental components meet at the *analytic point of interface* only in QUAN-*qual* design, when the results of the supplemental *qual* component are transformed numerically to fit in with the method used by the QUAN core component. Supplementary qualitative data are collected by intentionally including semistructured, open-ended questions within or at the end of a structured questionnaire or by using semistructured interviews. In this case, we may transform the supplemental components semistructured interview textual data to numerical data through processes of coding, and then move the transformed data into the QUAN core project as additional variables within quantitative analysis (see Chapter 9), or

2. *in the results narrative of the core component.* By *results narrative*, we mean the write-up of the core component findings. The narrative of the core component ALWAYS forms the base of the results, with the supplemental component embellishing or adding to certain information to special areas of the results (see Figure 5.1).

> Principle #8: Mixed method design is systematic.

> Principle #9: The two data sets remain separate until the *point of interface*.

> The point of interface is the position in the research process in which the two method meet.

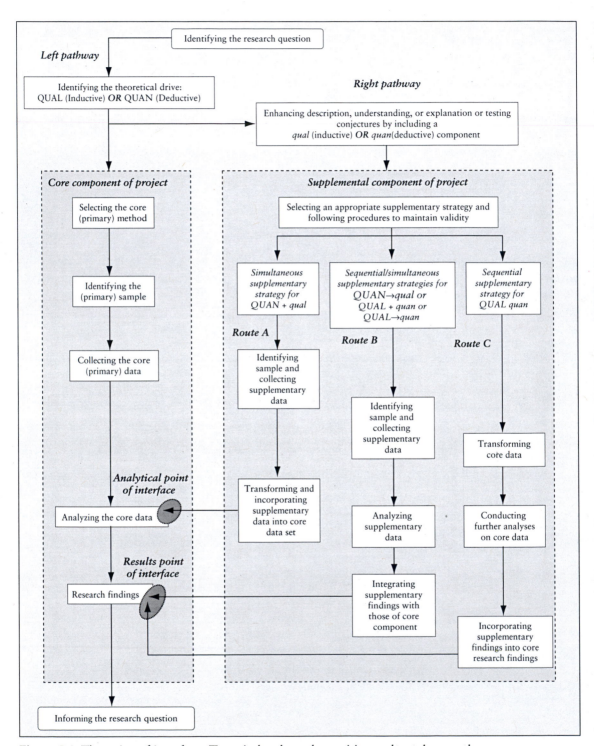

Figure 5.1 The point of interface: Two circles show the positions where the two data sets meet

It is important to note that the integration of the transformed supplementary data into the core data set is the most difficult integration point from a methodological perspective. Such integration occurs with only one design: QUAN + *qual*, when the *qual* component meets certain criteria. With all other designs (and with QUAN + *qual* when the *qual* method does not meet the necessary criteria), the integration point is in the results narrative. In the QUAN + *qual* design, the transformation of *qual* data and the incorporation of these data into the QUAN component may only occur in the presence of two design conditions:

1. *The sample size of the* qual *component must be the same as sample the* QUAN *component—and preferably using the same subjects.* This puts some limitations on the type of qualitative data that may be collected in the *qual* component, for the quantitative sample usually is much larger than is normally required for qualitative researcher. Depending on the *qual* methods used, the *qual* supplemental component may consist of open-ended questions within a quantitative survey, or may consist of a semistructured questionnaire.

2. *All of the qualitative participants must be asked the same question(s) in the same order.* Thus, this can only be done with the two of the designs mentioned above—open-ended questions in a quantitative survey or a semistructured interview design. With qualitative research that uses *un*structured interviews—a design used, for instance in ethnography or grounded theory—a design in which the researcher has been learning about the phenomenon as the research progresses, the interviews change over the course of the study. In the beginning, the researcher asks very broad questions, learning generally about the topic, but not necessarily seeking in-depth information. As the study progresses, the researcher pursues certain topics in depth, so that the interview questions change and become increasingly narrow specialized. The interview questions used later in the study elicit different information than those asked at the beginning of the study, so the responses cannot be combined or used comparatively. Characteristics or features within unstructured interviews cannot be counted across participants because the participants interviewed at different times may not have been asked the questions being tabulated.

Focus groups used in the supplemental component do not meet the two necessary criteria list above. In focus group interviews, the moderator poses questions for discussion and all of the members of the focus group do not necessarily answer the questions posed. Thus, the researcher does not know if all of the participant agree or disagree with a certain position; the responses to a certain questions cannot be tabulated or coded so that the results can be transformed numerically. This characteristic is extremely important.

Table 5.1 QUAN + *qual* designs: *qual* strategies that may and may not be used with an analytic point of interface

qual strategies that may be used with the analytic point of interface	*qual* strategies that cannot be used with the analytic point of interface
Semistructured interviews (pre-prepared, open-ended questions)	Unstructured interviews (one "grand tour" question is asked; the researcher assumes a listening stance)
Open-ended questions embedded within an QUAN survey	Conversational interviews (the researcher dialogues with participant)
	Guided interviews (approximately 6–10 questions are asked to elicit a story or account in a certain form)
	Phenomenological conversations (the researcher converses with participants, and even contribute his or her own story/experiences)
	Focus group interviews (moderator stimulates discussion of approximately 6–8 respondents, using guiding questions)
	Participant observation (unstructured observations recorded as field notes)
	A single open-ended question at the end of the questionnaire

In Table 5.1, we list the *qual* supplementary strategies of QUAN + *qual* that can and cannot be used to perform a textual to numerical conversion, and incorporate the results into the analytic point of interface. In Table 5.1, the anomaly is the open-ended question at the end of the survey. This question meets the two criteria given above in that it is asked of all participants. The problem with an open-ended question at the end of the survey is that it is too open. Usually this question is something like: "Do you have anything to add?" and the respondent can write about anything. When the researcher codes these responses, the fact the respondent could write about anything means that he or she does. This produces too many codes for a single variable to be amenable for the analysis—unless the researcher codes the responses very generally (they "like it" or they "did not like it"), and usually this item is not needed to get this information.

QUAN + *qual*: Analysis as *the Point of Interface* for *qual* Supplemental Component Data

To meet the above criteria for qualitative questions to be asked of all participants, use semistructured interviews or place semistructured questions within a quantitative survey. Because semistructured questions are open ended, they meet qualitative criteria of induction; they are asked of all participants and can therefore be administered to a larger sample. At the same time, they are frequently responded to without pages of discussion. These relatively short responses make them amenable to coding. Because the topics—and the content of the interview—are controlled by the researcher, they are more "efficient" than unstructured stories. Provided they are eliciting the necessary information required for the study, they can be administered to a relatively large sample. When designing these semistructured questions, however, the researcher should ensure the participants answer every question, otherwise missing data will become a problem when the data are transformed, moved into the quantitative component as a new variable, and analyzed quantitatively.

Must *all* of the participants have answered *all* of the questions? Depending the sample size, most can tolerate some missing data, but it depends on the question. Clearly if there is a lot of missing data, it will not be worthwhile transforming the item. Probably before you spend too much time with the item, you should obtain a statistical consultation.

Methods for the conversion of textual data to numerical data are well described in the literature and will be described in Chapter 9. Once data have been transcribed into numerical data, variables are created in the quantitative data set, and these numerical (and formally qualitative) data are entered.

The Results Section as the Point of Interface

When integrating results from the core and supplemental component, it is important to identify for the reader which results come from the core and the supplemental component of the study, so that the results narrative is never a "mishmash" with data completely integrated. It is must always be clear which data set the researcher is discussing. The important principle of *keeping both methodological components separate until the point of interface* is essential for maintaining validity.

With QUAL + *quan* or QUAN + *quan*, or QUAL + *qual* designs and QUAN + *qual* design that are unsuitable for transformation in the analytic point of interface (such as those with focus groups or unstructured interviews in which the participants have not all been asked the same questions in the same order), the point of interface usually occurs in the *results* section of the article or report. The researcher completes the analysis of the both core and the supplemental components and then brings the findings of the two methods together by incorporating the findings of the supplemental study into the narrative writing of the core results. Although this may occur a number of ways, for the sake of clarity and critical reviewers, it is important to "tag" or to label findings so that the source of each of the findings may be identified with the respective component of the study, and linked back to the respective component. We disagree with Sandelowski (2007) who suggests that results appear untagged, as an eloquent narrative. Rather, results MUST be linked to their source—you are writing RESULTS, not fiction. The processes or structures of analysis that make each method distinct, their source, and the perspective of the participants or the researcher, must always be evident.

When making decisions about combining the results of a core and a supplementary component, one *first* considers *the research question*. Recall that the core component addresses the majority of the research question and dictates the theoretical drive of the project. Therefore, as previously mentioned, this component usually forms the base, or the foundation, of the outline for presenting the results; the findings from the supplemental component adds descriptive detail at pertinent points in the narrative, or add paragraphs to expand on particular points.

A *second* consideration is the *form of the findings* derived from each method. For instance, quantitative studies provide information about categories or variables and their relationships, but do not provide qualitative descriptive data about what something *is*, and its meaning. Quantitative data provide detail about how much, how many, or what relations exist between concepts in the qualitative study. Phenomenological findings offer in-depth descriptions about particular aspects of the study, but do not show, as does grounded theory, how the phenomenon changes over time. Thus, the form of the findings dictate how the core and supplemental project it together, to form the narrative.

QUAL Core, *quan* Supplemental (QUAL-*quan*)

When we have a qualitative core, we already have, from the analysis of the QUAL unstructured interviews, a narrative, or from QUAL semistructured interviews, we already have qualitative descriptions by question. This narrative, or these descriptions, forms the *base* of the findings as the point of interface into which the *quan* findings fit. By this we mean that in the point of interface, the *quan* data from the quantitative analysis are inserted in the correct position into the core qualitative descriptive narrative.

QUAN—>*qual*
Examples of research using these designs are

- a survey followed by several focus groups
- a physiological study followed by a group of unstructured interviews
- a questionnaire study followed by participant observations

The QUAN—>*qual* study is usually conducted when the results of a quantitative study leave questions unanswered or important additional questions arise, or when, following the analysis of a quantitative data, surprises in the analysis that cannot be explained theoretically are noted. In all of these situations, a supplemental qualitative sample is drawn and unstructured interviews or observations are conducted until the researcher is confident of the results and the questions are answered. If a separate sample is drawn as in QUAN—>*qual* design, care must be taken to ensure that the participants are from the same population as the quantitative sample was obtained. In this case, the quantitative findings form the basis of the results narrative and the researcher may have even already drafted the results before recognizing the gaps that the qualitative study then addressed. This means that in the point of interface, the quantitative findings form the basis for the results, with the qualitative embellishing descriptions fitting in whenever necessary. As noted above, the analysis of the qualitative and quantitative results are presented in separate components.

QUAN-*quan*
Examples of QUAN + *quan* design would be

- a questionnaire design with a simultaneous concurrent physiological measurements
- a survey design with quantitative measure of anxiety
- quantitative observational measures with cost analysis

Occasionally, when conducting a quantitative project, it is recognized that additional data may be needed. If all the participants are still available and the second quantitative instrument may be administered to the entire sample, this is not considered a mixed method design.

However, if the quantitative data have been analyzed and another gap has been noted, it may be necessary to draw another sample and administer the supplemental instrument. In this case, the supplemental sample may or may not be equal in size as the quantitative core sample and this is a decision that must be made by the researchers. Because the two samples are from different sources, you have a mixed method design.

QUAN—>*qual* results narrative
If the quantitative core study has already been analyzed, the *qual* design is always sequential (QUAN—>*quan*). The point of interface, therefore, is always in the results narrative. Usually, this is written up with separate paragraphs addressing the separate findings. For example, in a QUAN—>*qual* study, Sosu, McWilliam, and Gray (2008) explored teachers' commitment to environmental education. They conducted a survey of teachers to explore significant factors that determine commitment and interviewed teachers regarding environmental education. (Although some of the multivariate questions stimulated interview

questions, the authors state that a part of the analysis was conducted simultaneously.)

The quantitative data from the survey (which provide breadth) are presented first, with the authors presenting the main findings in a table and a paragraph discussing the results. They then used "soft systems methodology" to develop a theoretical model.

The qualitative interview findings (which provided depth to the study) are presented in a separate section and organized into two sections or paragraphs: (1) "Perceived constraints to environmental education" and (2) "Current motivating factors" and "Results from the systems-thinking phase." Although this article was actually a publication explaining the research design (and the discussion discussed the design rather than the results of the study), the separation of the two components illustrated the problems of integrating quantitative and qualitative findings in the same study.

Endpoint

Despite efforts to merge or to integrate the qualitative and quantitative components of a mixed method study, the analysis is always conducted separately, and the logical place for the integration to occur is in the write-up of results. However, such integration is difficult to find. Perhaps some of the inhibitory factors come from reviewers who, when evaluating the article, need to be able to track the results from each component. Perhaps the cause is simply because writing separate components is neater, cleaner, and easier than merging sets of findings that, although complementary, do not fit easily together. There is some evidence that this will change with determined efforts of committed mixed methods researchers, and challenges from methodologists (Bryman, 2006b), but in the meantime, it is difficult to locate examples.

6

Sampling for Mixed Method Designs

In Chapter 2, we pointed out the problems involved with sampling in mixed method research, especially when the components use strategies from different paradigms. The major difficulty occurs when the project is qualitatively-driven and the supplemental component quantitative (QUAL-*quan*). In this case, the sample for the core component is too small and lacks randomization, and therefore does not meet quantitative requirements of the supplemental component. When the project is quantitatively-driven and the supplemental component qualitative (QUAN-*qual*), the sample for the quantitative core component is too large and lacks purposive selection and therefore does not meet the qualitative requirements necessary for the qualitative supplemental component. Except in certain circumstances when these limitations can be surmounted, additional samples must be drawn for the supplemental component. First, however, we will describe the sampling procedures in qualitative and quantitative paradigms.

Principle #7: Sampling must be compatible with the assumptions belonging to the method or strategy that it serves.

Sampling for Qualitative Designs

Sampling, that is, deciding who should be interviewed or observed, is a significant issue in qualitative inquiry. To be able to purposefully select participants for the study, you must be familiar with the knowledge and experiences of the potential participants. Also, the interviewing or observational skills of the researcher influences the nature of the data, the scope of the study, the depth of meaning identified, the complexity of the interpretation obtained, and the rate at which saturation is obtained. Although much has been written about the strategies for, and types of, sampling to be used at the beginning of a project, sampling strategies to be used when analysis is developing have been relatively ignored. Researchers must scope the domain by sampling for variation, to theoretically sample (according to the needs of the developing theory [Glaser, 1978]), and to continue sampling until saturation occurs.

> A qualitative sample is representative of the phenomenon.

Appropriate qualitative sampling is determined by the representativeness of the phenomena under study. Because the researchers are interested in identifying meaning, and the characteristics of phenomena, they must know something about the participants to select the best person to be in the study. Random selection does not ensure that the most appropriate individuals will be chosen. The participants' knowledge about the phenomenon or experience is the first criterion considered, but other characteristics such as the "qualities of a good informant" (Spradley, 1979) must also be taken into account. A participant to be interviewed must:

- have the necessary experiences or information;
- be willing to participate and have available time; and
- be articulate, expressive, and reflective

The above participant characteristics make the sample *appropriate*; qualitative *adequacy* is obtained by considering, on an ongoing basis, if the researcher has enough information about the topic to enable data to reach redundancy or *saturation*. To achieve this, the researcher keeps building the sample and analyzing data until he or she has comprehensive knowledge about the topic and no new information emerges when additional participants are interviewed or observed.

How many participants should be in a study cannot be predetermined and depends on the quality of the data and the simplicity or complexity of the information, with a greater number of participants being required if the quality of the interviews is poor or if the topic is complex.

The other consideration is that different qualitative methods require different amounts of data per participant, and there is an inverse relationship between the amount of data required from each participant and the number of participants. For instance, phenomenology, which may include three, six, or even more unstructured conversations per participant, may have fewer than six participants in the study. Grounded theory may have one or two interviews per participant and may have 30 or 40 participants in the study. At the extreme, semistructured interviews require a minimum of 30 participants, and as the data are easy to handle, often have more than 100—especially if the researcher intends to code and transform data numerically, to publish, for instance, mean scores and non-parametric statistics.

Major sampling strategies for qualitative inquiry are:

- *a convenience sample*: The investigator advertises for volunteers, invites the first group of people who meet the criteria, or uses a *total sample*: that is, all those who are present.
- *a quota sample*: In this sample, the investigator creates a sampling frame of two or more characteristics, with the minimum number of participants in each cell. For instance, the sampling frame developed to solicit adolescents, and organized by age

(10–13, 14–16, 17–19 years) by gender (males and females). This would give a total of six cells. The researcher may decide that five participants in each are necessary, giving a total of 30 participants.

- *a nominated (snowball) sample*: This design is used when participants know each other, but the research may have difficulty in identifying them. After the first person is interviewed, he or she then identifies and invites the next person to be in the study.

- *sampling for variation*: This method of sampling is used early in the investigation, when determining the scope of the study. The researcher deliberately selects participants who are different from each other according to certain characteristics, until whatever the researcher is interested in is weak or no longer present. In this way, the researcher identifies the boundaries and the major characteristics of the phenomenon.

- *homogeneous sample*: This design looks at participants with similar characteristics, in an attempt to reach saturation.

- *negative case sampling*: Participants who have certain minority characteristics are deliberately sought to increase understanding about uncommon features.

- *theoretical sampling*: As analysis proceeds, and various components of the developing theory need to be saturated, or if some areas appear thin, these requirements indicate what the characteristics of participants should be for subsequent interviews. Thus, participants are deliberately sought on an ongoing basis according to the needs of the analysis.

Sampling for the Quantitative Design

In quantitative inquiry, it is important that the sample be *representative of the population*. This is done primarily by: (1) delimiting the population; (2) ensuring that all members of the population have equal opportunity to be in the sample; and (3) making sure the sample will be of adequate size for the number of variables. As a rough guide, Teddlie and Yu (2007) note this is generally $n=50$ for representativeness.

If a sample is drawn from an appropriate population using techniques of randomization, the assumption is that the sample will be representative of that population—that there will be no bias. Adequacy is ensured by sample size—there should be an adequate number participants according to the demand of the research—usually according to the number of variables or, if it is an experimental design, according to power calculations based on expected differences between the experimental and control groups. As variables cluster according to the shape of a bell curve or normal distribution clustered about the mean and reducing in number toward the tails of the curve, researchers can quickly ensure that the sample is not skewed or biased. If, however, the distribution is skewed in the population, this distribution should be also reflected in the sample.

In addition to the *random sample*, other sampling strategies used in quantitative research are as follows:

A *stratified random sample*: Using this method, the groups of interest are sorted according to some characteristics of interest (such as age and gender) and the subjects are selected from these subgroups randomly.

A *cluster random sample*: When using cluster sampling, the sample unit is naturally occurring groups, which are then selected randomly.

Commonalities in Sampling

Despite the differences in sampling methods between the qualitative and quantitative paradigms, sampling methods are intended to:

- make the research optimally efficient, while
- maximizing validity, according to the adequacy and appropriateness of the sample.

If the researcher must violate the basic rules for sampling, it must be done with awareness of the risk to the project as a whole. These decisions must be made consciously, in full assessment of the cost—for sampling often involves some type of compromise.

What Are These Decisions?

Qualitative and quantitative samples have different rules, and as their data are in different forms (numerical and textual). Additionally, the way you are thinking in each project is different (deductively and inductively). When thinking about your research methods:

1. Identify methodological assumptions:

   - What is the nature of the phenomena under investigation? In qualitative research, consider their level of abstraction, complexity, and scope. With projects that have a quantitative theoretical drive, consider if the phenomena are quantifiable and, if so, how they are.
   - How will you obtain an appropriate and adequate sample as needed for your method?
   - What are the analytic assumptions associated with your selected method? (If the project is qualitative, think of the type of interview; if the project is quantitative, consider the level of data required for analysis, and so forth.)

2. Determine appropriateness and adequacy of supplemental component:
   - How complete is this component? Recall that by definition, supplemental components cannot stand on their own and are only interpretable in the context of the whole study and as they contribute to the core component.

Determine the degree of methodological fit and substantive relevance of the supplemental component to the project. For instance, if your supplementary component for a QUAN-*qual* design is methodologically a good fit with the quantitative main study, qualitative data may be transformed to numeric data and moved into the quantitative analytic core.

In the next sections, we explore sampling designs and decisions that must be made during the conduct of the major mixed method designs.

QUAL Sampling Designs

QUAL + *quan*

Depending on the type of qualitative method that forms the core component, in a qualitatively-driven design that is combined with a simultaneous quantitative supplement component, the core qualitative sample is not usually suitable for use with the quantitative supplemental component (see Figure 6.1). In QUAL + *quan* design, the qualitative core component requires a small, purposefully selected sample that will provide rich description of the phenomenon. Therefore, the qualitative sample does not meet the criteria of size (it is not large enough) and randomization required for the quantitative supplemental component.

First, consider the purpose and the methodological assumptions underlying the quantitative supplemental component. Are you measuring characteristics in the qualitative sample to add to the description? If so, then any quantitative instrument used to measure characteristics of a small qualitative sample must have standardized external norms against which the researcher can compare the scores obtained on the quantitative instrument. Because of the intentional bias of the qualitative sample, scores are virtually meaningless in the absence of such external norms. Follow the flow chart for Figure 6.1.

The first decision (inside the diamond) is:

Does the quantitative instrument have external norms? If "yes," then

- Use the qualitative sample for quantitative measurement, using standardized instruments. Then, to interpret these scores, compare each person's score obtained in the small qualitative sample with the external norms obtained by other researchers who developed the scale. Because these norms were established using a large sample, the researcher may then determine how each person's score compares with the average person's score. These results may be used to enhance the description of the qualitative sample, and be written into the study's findings.

If there is not an instrument with external norms (Figure 6.1, left pathway):

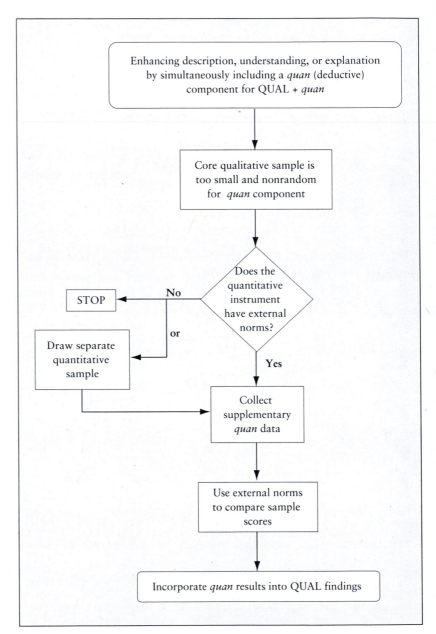

Figure 6.1 Sampling issues for QUAL + *quan* mixed method designs

- Pull a separate sample of participants from the population (using random selection) and analyze it using descriptive techniques. In this way, the quantitative sample will be large enough to analyze using descriptive statistics (most authors state that the minimum sample size to calculate a mean score is 30 (Pett, 1997).

If you want to administer the instrument to the qualitative sample, albeit with its limitations for quantitative measurement, administer the instrument to the total sample. Then, with the total sample scores, use nonparametric statistics and interpret the results cautiously.

If you chose to do none of the above,

- STOP! And rethink the design.

QUAL—>*quan*

Careful consideration of sampling issues that may occur for QUAL—> *quan* designs are crucial for maintaining validity. If a researcher is using a supplemental data collection strategy (Figure 6.2) and needs to measure some quantifiable aspects of a phenomenon once the qualitative core project is completed, a sampling problem may occur because the original participants in the qualitative sample may no longer be located.

Although we have noted that if the sample is not available you should stop, it is legitimate to administer the quantitative instrument to another randomly selected sample from a group that is equivalent to the qualitative sample. The same contingencies for interpreting the scores as in QUAL + *quan* design holds. If the sample is small, external norms must be used to interpret the scores obtained. These considerations are important, but if the instrument is appropriate for the purpose and has standardized norms, there is no inherent threat to validity in this design.

Another alternative is presented in Figure 6.3. Here, data from the QUAL component are transformed and analyzed in the *quan* component. Semistructured questionnaires are used most commonly with QUAL + *quan* design. Consider the assumptions inherent in semistructured interviews—they make the QUAL + *quan* design much easier: (1) In the QUAL core component, all participants are asked the same questions in the same order; and (2) the sample size is larger (at least 30).

Examples of designs that could be conducted using this design are:

- QUAL questionnaire + *quan* design, numerically transform and analyze
- QUAL videotapes of behaviors, —> behaviors coded according to some time frame to identify behavioral clusters (ethology).

Sampling and analysis issues may occur when the researcher is using a supplemental data analysis strategy for a *QUAL—>quan design* (Figure 6.3). The defining characteristics of the qualitative core method (i.e., the attributes that contribute to its validity), are usually at odds with the purpose and assumptions underlying the method from which the supplementary quantitative data analysis strategy is drawn. Most qualitative methods used in the core component require that data collection and analysis occur simultaneously, driving theoretical sampling. Further, conjectures worthy of testing may emerge at any point in the core data collection and analysis process, provided

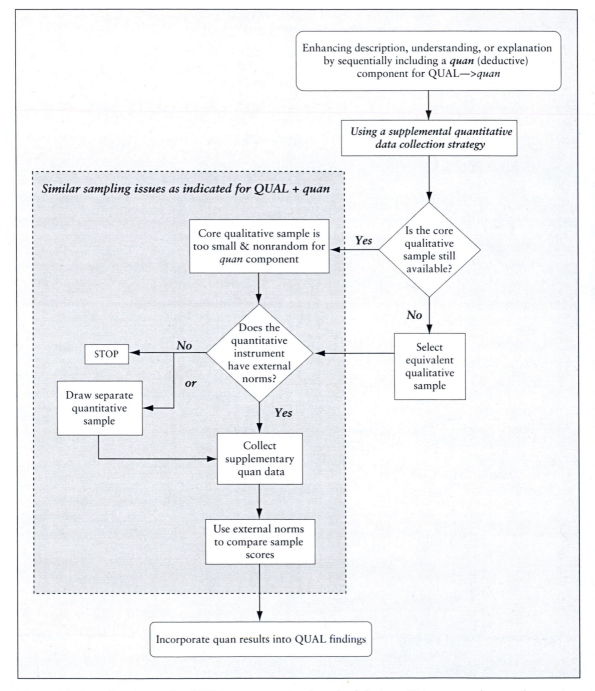

Figure 6.2 Sampling issues for QUAL—>*quan* mixed method designs (Using a supplemental quantitative data collection strategy)

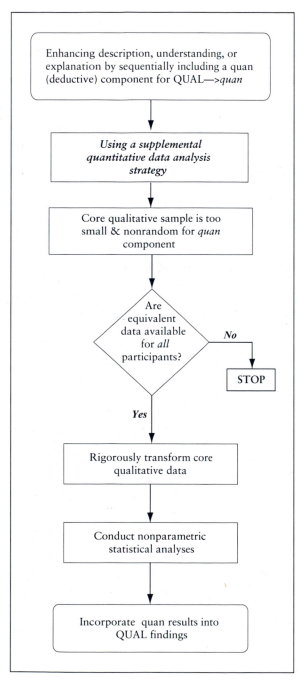

Figure 6.3 Sampling issues for QUAL—>*quan* mixed method designs (Using a supplemental quantitative data analysis strategy)

that categories are saturated. It is, therefore, crucial to consider the size and nature of the primary sample and whether equivalent data are available from all sample participants. Also, because the qualitative sample has been selected purposefully rather than randomly and the qualitative data are transformed into categorical variables, the researcher is restricted to using nonparametric statistical techniques for analyzing the transformed data. Even if the comparison is between two characteristics of participants within the sample, the lack of randomization of the qualitative sample means that generalizability of any quantified results must be regarded with caution.

Sampling for Quantitatively-Driven Projects

> A quantitative sample is representative of the population.

The primary concern for the quantitative sample is that it must be representative of the population and randomized—every person in the population has a equal opportunity to be selected for the sample—that is, the sample is appropriate. An adequate sample size ensures stability of the sample.

Sampling for QUAN + *qual* Simultaneous Designs

In QUAN + *qual* designs, the large, randomly selected quantitative sample is cumbersome for qualitative purposes (see Figure 6.4). If the quantitative sample is used for qualitative inquiry, the large number of participants overwhelms the analysis, and less frequently occurring data at the tails of the distribution are submerged. Further, because the participants have been selected randomly, they may be poor examples of whatever is being studied (and therefore poor participants), and a larger sample is needed to obtain the same richness of data. Therefore, qualitative data obtained as part of an otherwise quantitative instrument or questionnaire must be used cautiously to avoid threats to validity.

Given that the sample (both selection and size) for the supplemental qualitative component is the same as for the core quantitative component, if textual responses to semistructured, open-ended questions have been used, they may be transposed to quantitative data and incorporated into the core quantitative data set just *prior* to data analysis, consistent with the overall deductive theoretical drive of the project.

Analysis Issues for QUAN + *qual*

The supplemental qualitative component in this simultaneous QUAN design is usually semistructured interviews or open-ended questions within the core quantitative instrument. Again, this is because the questions are asked of all participants, in the same order. Because the questions require a relatively short answer, they can be administered to a relatively large sample—in fact, to the same participants.

Data are analyzed at the same time, once data collection is completed. Although qualitative content analysis can be used with these data, more frequently data are transformed numerically and the new

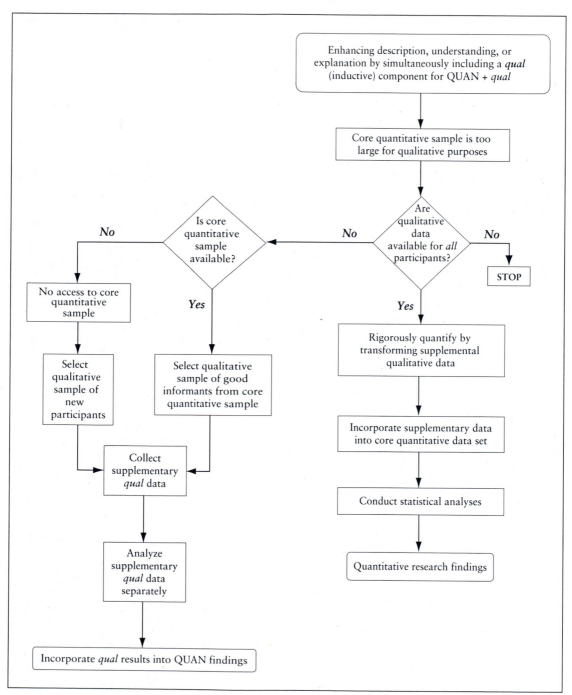

Figure 6.4 Sampling issues for QUAN + *qual* mixed method designs

variables are moved into the quantitative data set as new additional variables.

The methods for transposing these data have been rigorously described in texts, and we have outlined it in Figure 6.5. Analysis proceeds item by item across participants, in a process of content analysis, assigning numeric codes, establishing inter-rater reliability and moving the coded variable into the quantitative data set (see Chapter 9).

Sampling for QUAN-*qual* Sequential Designs

Sampling in a QUAN—>*qual* design is most difficult design (Figure 6.6). *If* the role of the supplemental component is to collect additional data to add description to the quantitative core component because of the sequential nature of the design, the core sample will no longer be accessible and a new sample will have to be obtained. Criteria for the qualitative purposeful selection of participants should be developed according to the theoretical needs of the study as indicated by the *quan* analysis. In addition, these criteria should also include criteria of a "good informant": ability to articulate, knowledge about interview topic, willingness to reflect on the topic, and time to participate (see Spradley, 1979). Therefore:

- *If* the researcher has access to the quantitative participants (for instance, research assistants who are collecting the quantitative data may be able to make referrals), then the principles of qualitative sampling should be followed to select a sample of good informants from the quantitative sample.

- If the researcher has *no* access to the quantitative participants (for instance, they cannot be traced or recalled), then the researcher has no alternative but to draw another sample, according to the needs of the qualitative supplementary component. Participants may be selected by such characteristics as scores achieved on the quantitative component, socioeconomic status, etc. Obviously, this sampling design is only slightly weaker than a multiple method design in which the sample would be that of a complete study, and the results would be rigorous enough to be published separately.

Last Word about Sampling

Teddlie and Yu (2007) remind us to describe the sample well enough so that the researcher is able to draw clear inferences from both the qualitative and the quantitative data. The conclusions of the study that are generalized to other groups must be credible and evident.

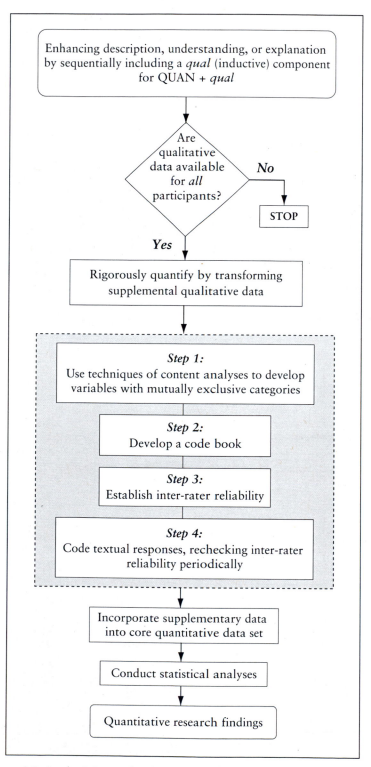

Figure 6.5 Analysis issues for QUAN + *qual* mixed method designs

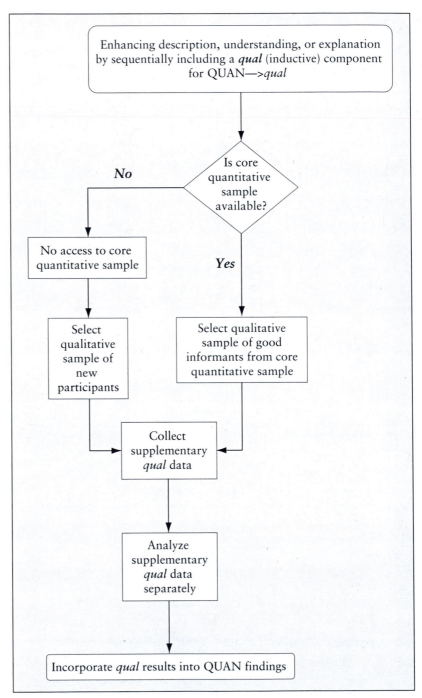

Figure 6.6 Sampling issues for QUAN—>*qual* mixed method designs

7

Planning a Mixed Method Project

We were going to call this chapter Writing the Mixed Method Proposal, but you have a lot of thinking and much planning to do *before* you write your proposal and put that thinking down on paper. And we wanted you to start this thinking now.

The Armchair Walkthrough

You have a topic—an interesting and exciting research problem. But the first thing we are going to ask you to do is to think about your topic as a single research design, because

- a mixed method study is almost twice as much work as a single method study, and
- a mixed method study is much more complex than a single method study, and because of this complexity, it is easier to mess things up.

Therefore, you need to be very certain that you actually have a mixed method project. Have you carefully considered the topic as a single method design using this or that method? Do you know what the limitations of your project are as a single method study? Are you ready and willing to risk—and put the effort into—a mixed method design? The best place to start is with an armchair walkthrough.

What Is an Armchair Walkthrough?

An armchair walkthrough (Mayan, 2009; Morse, 1994, 1999) is a very cheap, painless, quick, and smart way to envision all the alternatives for conducting your project. It enables you to envision the kinds of data you will need, to think about the types of analyses that may be conducted, and to understand the various possible outcomes.

Once you are familiar with your topic—that is, you have read extensively all of the materials you can get your hands on and even talked to others who have conducted studies in the area to get their advice, you are ready to do an armchair walkthrough. But while you do this, keep in mind that research is a coherent activity: The problem gives rise to the aims, which dictate the research question(s), which guide the design, which indicate which method(s) should be used, which dictate the analysis, which provide the results, which give you the implications. . . .

Now, to do an armchair walkthrough, you do not really need an armchair—it is optional—but you do need a space for undisturbed thinking in your favorite spot, with a pen and paper. A fire and a small glass of brandy might help, but a cliff above an ocean, a mountainside, or a spot by a lake may also be substituted. Someone we know always chooses a corner table at McDonalds and a large coffee. Whatever works for to help you with your thinking. . . .

Now—and this is the fun part—you are going to do a lot of "if" thinking:

If I ask this question, I will need to sample here from these folk, data will look like this-and-that, I will analyze it this way, and at the end of the day I will know thus-and-so.

You must mentally walk through the project asking as many questions as you can, and answering them using as many different methods—both qualitative and quantitative—that you can conceive. Write down the designs and anticipated results, so you can compare methods and outcomes.

Now, seriously consider the limitations of each of these "best" methods. Consider, *If I did this, I would know thus-and-so, but I still would not have information about this or that.*

Can you live with the limitations and restrictions of a single method design? If your answer is yes, then move forward with a single method design and do not read the rest of this book—at least not at this time.

If the answer is no, then consider doing two projects—one now and the second at the end of this project. The reason for this is that, by starting off small, you will have something publishable at the end of the small project. Earn your degree and do the second project during your postdoc. Living life in a multiple method research program is not so bad, and you can skip to Chapter 10—at least at this time.

But if you cannot accept the limitations that you can already envision with the single method project, if you can see where your research program is headed after this project, and you need more solutions more quickly than a single method project or a multiple method program will give you, if you are in a hurry to get through life, then a mixed method project may be for you.

Back to the drawing board. . . .

This time, conduct the armchair walkthrough using several mixed method designs. The core component may be one of the single method designs you have already considered and the supplemental component designed to fill the gaps or capture the missing data noted earlier.

When "walking through" with a mixed method design, cost and effort are no restriction, so one should imagine the ideal project. This project should not be constrained by unavailable participants or nonresponses; it should not be limited by budgetary constraints or personnel, or by language or illiteracy. Plan the best conceivable project and then later compromise the design if you really have to, when reality intervenes.

Now Prepare Your Own Flowchart

Once you have the best project conceptualized, move toward writing the proposal. First, diagram your design. Draw it as a flowchart, putting as many design features on the flow chart as possible. Put in the question that the core component will answer and the question that the supplemental component will address. Show the theoretical drive and the core and supplemental components. Put your sample onto the flowchart. Show quantitative instruments (if any) and other measures and how these data will be interpreted. Qualitative sample? Kinds of data—interviews? Observations? How will these data be analyzed? Where is the point of interface between the core and the supplemental components?

> Diagramming simplifies conceptualizing your project.

Self-Audit

Now audit yourself: Do you really need all of those sets of data sets?

Remember, parsimony is perfection. Making more work is not smart, and the risk of validity violations increases as you add supplemental components.

Now, ensure that you follow Principle #10, and adhere to the methodological assumptions of the core method,

Look at your research question, and ask:

Is the question exploratory or descriptive?

If so, the *theoretical drive* of your project is inductive, and your *core* method—that is the main method, is the one that is complete—is presented in the left-hand pathway in our figures, with the supplementary project in the right-hand pathway.

Is the question quantitative? Are you asking how much or how many? Is it a question that tests some hypothesis or theory?

If so, your theoretical drive will be deductive, and the core method or the complete method used in your study, quantitative. Again, it is diagrammed as the left pathway.

Think long and hard about the nature of the sample for each component. How will you locate the sample? What are the limitations of the sample? Will it be adequate and appropriate?

Ask:

- What is the nature of the core sample?
- Can the supplementary component of the project use the same sample (or subsample of the study population) as the core, or does it require a new sample?

> Principle #1: Work with as few data sets as possible (or, keep it simple!)

> Principle #10: Adhere to the methodological assumptions of the core method.

> Audit your own design.

> Principle #7: Sampling must be compatible with the assumptions belonging to the method or strategy it serves.

- Do your methods of recruitment violate any assumptions for the method that you will be using the sample?
- How will appropriateness and adequacy of a new or supplementary sample be assured?

Now, consider the interaction of the two components:

Principle #6: Carefully consider the pacing of the components.

- Are the analytical assumptions underlying the data involved in the core component of the project and supplementary strategies compatible with one another?
- Ask: What else do I need to know to be able to answer this question? Will it be conducted at the same time as the core component (simultaneous), or after the core component is completed (sequential)?
- Is the project optimally paced? Will both components be able to support each other, or are they appropriately separate?
- Consider how the two studies will meet. Most frequently this is when the researcher writes up the finding, but in certain circumstances this may be during the analysis.

Can you justify (or defend) your decisions? This preparation enables you to see the project in its entirety, to discover and correct any pit falls.

Compensating for Researcher Limitations

The difficulty with writing a mixed method proposal is that we are expected to go beyond our comfort zones and become super versatile researchers, adept in both research paradigms and in many types of research methods. But to gain a fundable score, we must meet the criteria of both qualitative and quantitative reviewers—that is, to please the entire review committee. This will not be a situation in which members without the expertise will defer to the judgment of other members. It is a situation in which everyone will know something, and everyone will have his or her own private quirk—some indicator or other that they demand to see in a good proposal. And, if these reviewers do not know something, they will be expecting the investigator to inform them, with the rationale. No additional pages are given for such proposals; you must simply exude excellence—write tightly, clearly, logically, and comprehensively with confidence.

Writing the Mixed Method Project

The advantage of preparing a mixed method proposal (rather than using an emergent design) is that the researcher can recruit the necessary qualitative and quantitative expertise, obtain the necessary approvals, make plans for a complete sampling and data management system, recognize how the data and analyses will complement each other and foresee how the results will be enriched with the combination of the two methods, and, finally and most importantly, request adequate funding in the proposal for conducting both methods.

Design Considerations

Remember, in mixed method design, the two methods designated to address the research questions are never of equal weight—they do not make an equivalent contribution to the research design. By definition, one method answers the questions best.

Consider the degree of completion of the supplementary project: You may not be able to make this decision ahead of time, especially if your research has a qualitative supplement or is an emergent design. The amount of data you collect for the supplementary component will, of course, depend on what you are asking. However, it is recommended that the qualitative supplemental project be kept simple, because its purpose is generally specific and targeted. (If you need more from the supplemental project, perhaps your supplemental component is actually a single subject design.)

Designs that "Emerge"

As mentioned, the need for conducting a mixed method design may also *emerge* after the project has started. Planning for the supplemental component may occur midway during a project when investigators encounter something important and unexpected and want to explore the phenomenon during this project (and therefore conduct simultaneous mixed methods). Alternatively, researchers may encounter unexpected findings at the end of the data analysis and seek some explanation for those findings in the present study, thereby converting the present study into a sequential mixed methods design. Obviously, the emergent design has advantages for the investigator in the time saved for the overall research program and benefits such as the possible availability of the sample, but it causes a scurry in the research team. The researcher will have to obtain ethics and funding agency approvals for the changed protocol, adequate funding for the change (which may be available or a supplement will have to be requested), and even a time extension for the grant. But the advantages may well override these difficulties: The researcher will have a much stronger publication and a better proposal for the next application.

Remember, research is always a puzzle waiting to be solved, and the better the solution—or contribution—the better!

Forming a Research Team

With the increasing appearance of mixed methods grants, qualitative researchers often find themselves as principal investigators or as team members on a grant preparing a mixed method proposal. As qualitative researchers, interested in qualitatively-driven proposals, we see a new standard appearing that bears some comment. That is, the review committees considering these proposals demand equally rigorous standards for both components—even if the project is designed sequentially. Although the quantitative component will be developed from the findings of the qualitative, and not commence until year 3, it must be as equally well developed as a single method quantitative project.

In other words, these proposals must be exemplary in both qualitative and quantitative methods (Morse, 2008). Review committees will not accept the uncertainties within the quantitative components that researchers will know they will have, even if it is a qualitatively-driven project. Yes—there will be a lot of *if* statements in your proposal, and this will be a necessity. But the golden rule stands—even *if* you do not know exactly *what* you will find, write how you will proceed methodologically as completely as possible.

First, if you are strong qualitatively, but not as strong as desired quantitatively (or are perceived as such), form a strong and well-balanced team. Find a good quantitative co-investigator (or even co-PI), who can increase his or her time contribution as the project progresses and the methods change. Have that person write the quantitative component, *as if* this were a quantitative application. If you have the quantitative skills, and consider your weaknesses to be qualitative, the reverse is true: Find a strong qualitative collaborator.

Second, the qualitative component must be extremely strong. Does the literature review place the project in a context that demonstrates that emerging knowledge is needed? Will such processes move the field forward? MUST the problem be tackled this way? Does it state clearly that the "state of the art" does not lend itself to beginning quantitatively? Now, at the same time, in the same literature review, you must be confident (and convey this confidence to the reviewer) that you will be able to find the information that will enable you to move quickly into the quantitative component.

What is the nature of the quantitative component? If it is a survey, or it is developing some type of instrument that will be based on the qualitative data and the methods to be used have been clearly developed, your proposal should be straightforward. But do not cut any corners, and when writing, give equal weight (and space) to the quantitative methods. Tell reviewers how you will develop the instrument—what the anticipated domains are, how you will develop the items, how you will pretest and ensure validity, and so forth. But do not stop there. Tell them you will obtain institutional review board approval for this component. Tell them how you will calculate your sample size, how you will obtain your sample, and what the demographic characteristics will be. Tell the reviewers what you will do about low response rate, missing data, and all of those difficulties that one encounters. Tell them how you will analyze and interpret these data. Finally, do not forget the great "so what," and boast about the overall significance of such a study.

Checkpoints for Writing the Proposal

Once you know what you plan to do, you may write.

Developing research question(s): Tighten your question. The project must clearly state the purpose or the desired outcome of the project, and it is from this aim that the theoretical drive should be evident. Ask: "Am I working in an exploratory mode or a theory testing mode?" "How much is known about this topic?" "Do I have any serious concerns or questions about the literature?" If you do have serious concerns about the literature, it is possible that, although there may be a reasonable amount written about your topic, you may have reservations serious enough to begin your project qualitatively. Of course, some aims will be somewhere between these two poles of knowing much and knowing little. The choice of conducting a qualitatively or a quantitatively-driven project will be your decision to select and justify.

Next, the research question—or questions—are identified, and the methods selected extend directly from the way the question is stated. Now, examine these questions to determine if the theoretical drive is inductive or deductive, and whether your study will be QUAL or QUAN. Explore the supplemental components: Is the supplemental component well justified? Does it extend logically from the research question(s)? Is there an excellent fit between the information sought, the sampling frame, and the methods?

Justify and explicate your analysis plan. Make certain it is intelligible to someone unfamiliar with the methods and design. Check the point of interface and plans for the combining of the data sets. Are plans for the joining of the results narrative clearly stated, and plans for dissemination/application well developed?

Once you are satisfied with the proposal, have it edited and reviewed by your peers. Then, when all of the revisions are complete, submit your proposal!

Good luck!

8

Qualitatively-Driven Mixed Method Designs

In this chapter, we discuss research in which the core component is qualitative and has an inductive theoretical drive. It is not our intent to provide a lot of detail about how to conduct the core method (for this would expand the book into a qualitative text) should you require more information about qualitative methods, but we have provided some guidance and external references. Here, we will focus on the ways qualitative studies may be expanded to include a quantitative component, or even a second qualitative component.

As mentioned earlier, because of problems with sampling that occur with the quantitative supplementary component, the QUAL-*quan* combination for mixed methods is probably the most difficult of all mixed method designs. The core component has a qualitative sample—one that is too small and violates the necessary principles of randomization, essential for the *quan* supplementary component. It is always necessary to be clear about what you are doing and why, and to recognize when and if you are *actually* using qualitative strategies and thinking inductively or working (albeit temporarily) in the supplementary component and thinking deductively. Keep these two processes—inductive and deductive thinking—as separate as possible, and this will reduce the risk of violating assumptions.

> Principle #11: The direction of theoretical drive is evident in the core component. But between the supplemental sample selection and the point of interface, the researcher must adhere to the paradigmatic assumptions of the supplemental method.

The Role of the Theoretical Drive

With qualitatively-driven projects, QUAL, the theoretical drive and the core component are inductive. That is, the overall drive is one of discovery, of exploration, as a means for finding something out. Even if the minor, supplemental component is deductive and quantitatively-driven (as in a QUAL-*quan* design), despite the quantitative supplementary component (and the fact that this component *will be conducted deductively*), the overall theoretical drive of the project *remains inductive*.

How does this appear in a study? First look at the research aims. They should clearly appear inductive. Remember, the research aim determines the overall inductive or deductive direction (drive) of the

> With QUAL-*quan* designs, even though the supplemental project is deductive, the overall theoretical drive remains inductive.

research project. However, the research question(s) (or sub-aims) may appear two-fold, with the major one for the qualitative core and a minor one addressing the quantitative component. The questions are generally placed at the end of the literature reviews and should be more specifically targeted to the individual strategies in the research design.

A QUAL—>*quan* research study about how political ads alienated college students (Parmelee, Perkins, & Sayre, 2007) had the following aim: "This study used a mixed method approach to explain how and why the political ads of the 2004 presidential candidates failed to engage youth" (p. 184). In this study, "three inter-related research questions are addressed:

- How does the interaction between audience-level and medical-based framing contribute to college students' interpretations of the messages found in political advertising?
- To what extent do those interpretations match the framing found in the ads from the 2004 U.S. presidential election?
- How can political ads be framed to better engage college students?" (p. 186)

Each of these three questions led directly to the design: Focus groups were conducted, providing college students with the opportunity to comment on eight presidential campaign ads, which asked: "In what ways have political ads successfully or unsuccessfully spoken to you in the past?" "How did the ads shown in the study speak to you?" "What would you do to make the political ads better engage college students?" (p. 188). Following this, the sequential quantitative phase, a content analysis of 118 images and issues in the Bush and Kerry TV ads was conducted to confirm and to elaborate on the qualitative findings (Parmelee, Perkinds, & Sayre, 2007, p. 189).

Sampling

Standard qualitative procedures are used to obtain the qualitative sample for the core component, according to the needs of the study (see Chapter 6). Initially, in qualitative inquiry, a small purposeful sample is drawn, and, later in the study, a theoretical sample. Problems in sampling with QUAL-*quan* studies arise when we consider the needs of the quantitative component, as the qualitative sample is inadequate, because of the small sample size and lack of randomization, for the requirements of most quantitative methods. The researcher has several choices for the quantitative supplementary component, depending on the *research purpose* (i.e., why you are adding the component):

1. *Use external norms*: If the purpose of the supplemental component is to add a quantitative measure of some dimension for each participant, then if the researcher selects a standardized measure with norms, the researcher simply administers a test or measure to each of the participants and interprets each result by comparing

it with the external normative scores. These results are added descriptively to the results narrative. For example, you may write: "The participants were highly anxious. When their scores on the anxiety scale were compared with standardized norms, all participants scored 2 standard deviations above the norm."

2. *Use the same sample*: If the qualitative sample is large enough (see Chapter 6), then the researcher may present the quantitative measure of the qualitative sample as frequencies. However, the researcher must remember that the sample was one of convenience and therefore may be biased. This will remain as a limitation of the study.

3. *Draw another sample*: If neither of the above alternatives is feasible or if it carries too much risk and threatens the validity of the study, then the researcher has no alternative but to draw another, larger sample for the quantitative supplement. Care must be made to make certain that the population from which the sample drawn is as similar to the qualitative sample's population as possible. This alternative is often used, however, as it has many advantages. The sample can be quantitatively adequate in size and randomly drawn. However, if a separate sample is drawn, the *point of interface* of the qualitative core and the quantitative supplementary component must, of course, be in the findings, with the results of both components integrated in the narrative.

Pacing

The two components of the qualitatively-driven mixed method design may be paced simultaneously or sequentially. *Simultaneous pacing* is essential if the design requires measurement of all of the same participants in both components, but if the *quan* supplementary component requires a separate sample, then the supplementary component may be paced simultaneously or sequentially, according to the researcher's preferences or resources.

Point of Interface

When the qualitatively-driven core component is used to explore or to describe a phenomenon, the point of interface of the quantitative supplementary component is almost always in the Results narrative. The qualitative findings form the theoretical frame of the results, and the quantitative description is used to expand certain details of these results.

Example

Let us continue with Parmelee, Perkinds, and Sayre's (2007) example about how political ads alienated college students. If we examine how the results narrative is presented, we see that the findings from the focus groups and the content analysis are presented separately within the results. For instance the paragraphs addressing the focus group findings are clearly marked as such ("Focus group participants felt. . ."

[p. 191]), as were content analysis findings. Although presented in separate paragraphs, these findings were clearly complementary, each contributing to the case the authors were making. This was reinforced and discussed further in the Discussion section (pp. 195–197).

Example: Parmelee, J. H., Perkins, S. C., & Sayre, J. J. (2007). "What about people our age?" Applying qualitative and quantitative methods to uncover how political ads alienate college students. *Journal of Mixed Methods Research*, *1*(2), 183–199.

Design	Theoretical drive: Inductive	Pacing: Sequential
	QUAL component: Focus groups	*quan* component:
	Point of Interface: Results	Content analysis

QUAL: The Qualitatively-Driven Core Component

Overview

Outlines for the major QUAL-*quan* design are shown in Figure 8.1. *Route A* shows the simultaneous QUAL + *quan* and the sequential QUAL—>*quan* design. Note that data for quantification occurs one of two ways: (1) collecting and analyzing new data to meet the needs of a quantitative measure (*Route A*); or (2) by using the qualitative core data *directly* and quantifying (transforming) these data. As discussed in Chapter 5, the *point of interface* for all QUAL designs is in the narrative of the *research findings*. Analytically, the qualitative and the quantitative pathways are conducted separately, in parallel (for simultaneous designs) and sequentially, following the completion of the QUAL analysis (but prior to writing it up) for simultaneous design.

If you are using simultaneous *quan* measure to enhance description, then you are bringing in measures to assess some qualities of the sample. As stated earlier, you must have external norms to compare the results, for the qualitative sample is usually too small to obtain meaningful group results. Additional samples are often drawn to confirm emerging hypotheses, for instance, to confirm an observation made in the small qualitative sample.

Sequential QUAL—>*quan* designs may be conducted with the same sample data or by drawing a new sample, although if the sample becomes large, the researcher may be moving into qualitatively-driven *multiple method* design. Each of these components will be discussed in the remainder of this chapter.

Methods

The major research methods used for the qualitative core components for QUAL-*quan* research, and the rational for adding the quantitative components, are shown in Figure 8.2. Although the qualitative core components *could* be published as is, the additional information

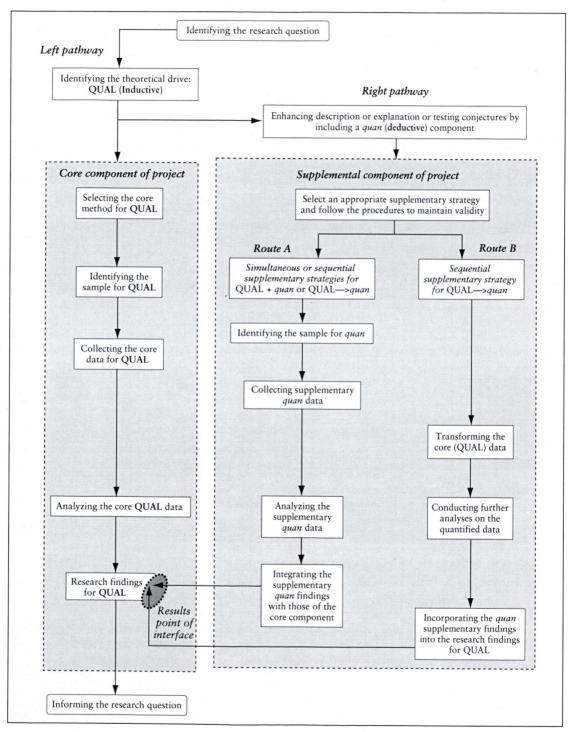

Figure 8.1 An overview of QUAL-*quan* mixed method designs

obtained from the simultaneous or sequential supplemental quantitative components give these projects something extra, an edge over the single method designs.

The QUAL (Qualitative) Core Component

Recall that the core component of the project is always complete and must be publishable on its own, without the supplemental components. Examples of the core *qualitative* method may be such methods as ethnography, grounded theory, phenomenology, narrative inquiry, focus groups, semistructured interview research, and so forth. These major methods will be described briefly below.

Focus Group Research

Focus groups are very efficient ways to elicit opinions or to rapidly develop a beginning understanding of an area. Basically, focus groups are a planned discussion among a group of people, led by a *facilitator*. The group participants (ideally consisting of six to eight people) are usually selected according to some criteria—they have had a certain experience in common (for instance, a child hospitalized with a certain illness), live in a certain district, are all of the same gender, similar age, and ethnic group, and so forth.

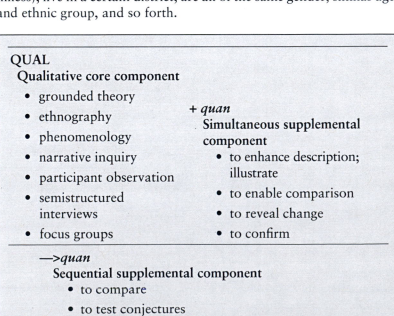

QUAL
Qualitative core component
- grounded theory
- ethnography
- phenomenology
- narrative inquiry
- participant observation
- semistructured interviews
- focus groups

+ *quan*
Simultaneous supplemental component
- to enhance description; illustrate
- to enable comparison
- to reveal change
- to confirm

—>*quan*
Sequential supplemental component
- to compare
- to test conjectures
- to identify patterns
- to determine distribution of QUAL findings in population*
- to test the emerging theory*

*These methods move the study design toward multiple-method design

Figure 8.2 Overview: Examples of QUAL-*quan* components

A trained facilitator leads the group discussion, and his or her role is to ask questions of the group and to stimulate discussion between the focus group members. Facilitators try for a balanced conversation, without letting any one member dominate the conversation; they try to draw out quiet members and let all opinions emerge in the discussion. In the process of stimulating discussion, additional questions emerge, and the facilitator is free to put these to the group. Examples of planned focus group questions are in the list below (List 8.1).

List 8.1. Example: The form of focus group questions

In a study to explore ways the certified nursing assistants from 16 nursing homes in Massachusetts make meaning of their work despite devaluation, lack of respect, physical and emotional demands, Pfefferle and Weinberg (2008) conducted 87 focus groups. They asked:

1. What do you like best about your job?
2. If you could change one thing about your job, besides being paid more, what would it be?
3. How would you describe the "feeling" in your facility?
4. How well do people work together?
5. What does management really care about here?

How many focus groups comprise a study? This depends on the nature and scope of the question, the amount of variety of information that emerges, the degree of uniformity of opinion or dissention surrounding the topic, and the purpose of the focus group component. If the focus groups are forming the core component of the QUAL mixed method study, the researcher must continue adding groups until adequate and appropriate data are obtained. The size of each group (i.e., the number of participants), is tricky—for if the groups are too small, the interaction may miss important variation; if they are too large, then everyone may not have not have the opportunity to present their opinion. But if the focus group participants are to answer questions that will form a solid theoretical core for the project, then the researcher must continue adding groups until those research goals are met.

Note that because all members of the group may not be explicitly asked every question, or may not answer every question, the researcher cannot count responses by participants. Focus groups are *not* the same as a survey.

Researchers often analyze the data using some form of content analysis, or analyze data by identifying themes. Focus groups are often used to develop a description of a particular topic or to develop a theoretical frame that will be used, for instance, in a survey. The categories are often used as theoretical constructs, which are operationalized into measurable items for a questionnaire. The focus group dialogue will give the researcher both the content and the language that may be used for item development, thereby increasing validity of the scale.

Importantly, because the subsequent quantitative component rests on the integrity of the QUAL focus group core component, these studies are qualitatively-driven, QUAL—>*quan* design, NOT *qual*—>QUAN. The theoretical drive is determined by the theoretical contribution and the way that the researcher is working conceptually, not by the component that appears to be the most work, takes the longest time to do, or is the most expensive. The theoretical drive is determined by the research question, involves the major theoretical contribution, and in this case, this is the development of the theoretical framework from the focus groups. All of the subsequent use of the results rests on the integrity of the qualitative core

---

Resources

Kruger, R. (2008). *Focus groups: A practical guide for applied research,* 4th ed. Thousand Oaks, Sage.
Barbour, R. (2007). *Doing focus groups.* Thousand Oaks, CA: Sage.

Semistructured Interviews

Semistructured interviews are used when the researcher knows enough about the topic (either from the literature or from previous research) to be able to:

- delineate the domain of the research, identify its boundaries, or know where the limits of the phenomenon are (i.e., what is and what is not an example of the phenomenon);
- identify all of the research areas or domains in all of its various types or kinds; and
- develop all of the questions pertaining to the phenomenon, but not necessarily know all of the possible responses.

Semistructured questionnaires are developed so that the question stems are presented in a logical order (either in a written questionnaire or when verbally presented to a participant in a face-to-face interview). The participant may then answer the question as freely as he or she pleases. If the questionnaire is presented verbally, the researcher may *probe* and ask for additional information "Tell me more. . ." or the probes may be written on a questionnaire as subquestions: "Please explain your answer..."

An example of a semistructured questionnaire is presented in List 8.2. This questionnaire was developed in a study to explore the risks to participants participating in qualitative research (Morse, Niehaus, & Varnhagen 2003), and the part of the questionnaire presented below refers to participants responding to unstructured, interactive interviews. Note that the research questions are designed to move through the domain systematically, so that the interview is controlled by the researcher, seeking targeted, specific information; although the participant has "freedom within limits" to express his or her opinions and tell of his or her experiences, the researcher keeps the participant "on track." The questions are "set" at the beginning of the study, so once the data collection has begun, the researcher cannot add or alter questions. All participants are therefore asked the same questions in the same order. In this example, standardized probes have been developed, but this is not always the case; the researcher is not necessarily restricted to the use of these probes.

List 8.2: Example: A Semistructured Questionnaire

1. Regarding *unstructured interactive interviews*:

    Describe the course of typical interviews.

    What is the typical response of participants during these interviews?

    Describe the typical responses of participants at the end of the interview.

    > Were there any incidents during your career as a qualitative researcher in which you perceived responses of participants to be *unexpected or extraordinary*?

    1.4.1 Briefly tell me more about the nature of these responses of participants.

    Negative responses:

    1.4.1.1 Please tell me more about the most worrisome participant response.

    > • *Probes:* If anything, what did you do?
    > What were the outcomes?
    > Do you have any regrets about anything you said or did? In what way?
    > What could be done to avoid incidents such as these?

    Positive responses:

    1.4.1.2 Please tell me about the most positive responses of participants.

    > • *Probes:* What did participants say?
    > What were the outcomes?
    > In your opinion, did the participant benefit from the interview?

    1.4.1.3 What do you do to mitigate risk for participants participating in this type of qualitative interviews?

Source: Risks to participants undergoing qualitative interviews: Perspectives of researchers, and research ethics boards [Proposal]. Funded by CIHR, Grant # 11669, J. Morse PI. In Morse, J. M., Niehaus, L., & Varnhagen 2003.

As mentioned, data collected by using semistructured questionnaires are analyzed at the end of data collection. They are analyzed all at once, item by item. The usual method is via some form of content analysis (see Hsieh & Shannon, 2005): All of the answers to item number 1.1, for example, are placed in the same file, and those "courses" of typical interviews sorted, so they may, if necessary be labeled and described.

Because every participant has been asked the same questions in the same order, this type of interview is amenable to *counting, by participant*. The different types of "courses of typical interviews" may be tabulated, the responses expressed as percentages (and other frequencies used, if desired) with the total N the number of participants. In this way, the researcher has the advantage of rich qualitative description, in addition to the numbers or percentages of each type of response. [Note: If a researcher is using semistructured interviews as the supplemental component of QUAN-*qual* design, the types of responses may even be coded and these codes moved into a quantitative data set as variables. We call this *textual—>numerical transformation*. This transformational procedure makes this type of interview very important for QUAN + *qual* mixed method design; it will be discussed in Chapter 9.]

Resources

Bartholomew, K., Henderson, A., & Marcia, J. E. (2000). Coded semistructured interviews in social psychology research in *Handbook of research in social and personality psychology*, H. T. Reis & C. Judd, eds. (pp. 286–321). New York: Cambridge University Press.

Richards, L., & Morse, J. M. (2007). *Readme first for a user's guide to qualitative methods*, 2nd ed. Thousand Oaks, CA: Sage.

Grounded Theory

Grounded theory, developed by Glaser and Strauss in 1967, is a method of developing midrange theory from data. It is a way of identifying what is *going on* or *what is happening* (or *has happened*) within a setting or around a particular event. It enables documentation of change and understanding of the processes central to that change. Grounded theory makes possible the identification and description of phenomena, their main attributes, and the social or social psychological processes involved as well as their interactions in the trajectory of change. It provides us with the tools needed to synthesize these data, and to develop concepts. Its power lies in the development of midrange theory; this makes it generalizable to other instances and to future instances (Morse et al., 2008).

Since its initial development in 1967, grounded theory as a method has evolved into several forms: Straussian grounded theory (led by Julie Corbin [Corbin & Strauss, 2008]), Glaserian grounded theory (Glaser, 1978; Stern, 2008), dimensional analysis (Bowers &

Schatzman, 2008; Schatzman, 1991), constructivist grounded theory (Charmaz, 2006, 2008), and situational analysis (Clarke, 2005, 2008). These variations and developments of grounded theory have a different purpose and different product, which have been recently clarified (Morse et al., 2008), so that it is no longer adequate to mention grounded theory without further qualification. However, there are several commonalities: All grounded theories consist of unstructured interviews; they use techniques to categorize data and to identify characteristics; and they are interested in interactions and process. Importantly, all types of grounded theory may use other data sources: observations, documents, and so forth. They usually have distinct strategies for data analysis—most commonly, constant comparison.

All types of grounded theory are individual methods in their own right. Therefore, if used in mixed method design, they must be used only as the core, and not as the supplementary component. Because grounded theory is a method, not a strategy, and is a complete method, if grounded theory is required as an accompanying method, the researcher must then be conducting a multiple method project.

Resources

Morse, J. M., Stern, P. N., Corbin, J., Bowers, B., Charmaz, K., & Clarke, A. (2008). *Grounded theory: The second generation*. Walnut Creek, CA: Left Coast Press.

Constructivist Grounded Theory

Charmaz, K. (2006). *Constructing grounded theory: A practical guide through qualitative analysis*. London: Sage.

Dimensional Analysis:

Bowers, B., & Schatzman, L. (2008). Dimensional analysis In *Grounded theory: The second generation*, Morse, J. M., Stern, P. N., Corbin, J., Bowers, B., Charmaz, K., & Clarke, A. (pp. 86–106). Walnut Creek, CA: Left Coast Press.

Glaserian Grounded Theory

Glaser, B. G. (1978). *Theoretical sensitivity*. Mill Valley, CA: Sociology Press.

Stern, P. N. (2008). Glaserian grounded theory. In *Grounded theory: The second generation*, J. M. Morse, P. N. Stern, J. Corbin, B. Bowers, K. Charmaz, & A. Clarke, eds. (pp. 55–65). Walnut Creek, CA: Left Coast Press.

Situated Grounded Theory

Clarke, A. E. (2005). *Situational analysis: Grounded theory after the postmodern turn*. Thousand Oaks, CA: Sage.

Straussian Grounded Theory

Corbin, J., & Strauss, A. (2008). *Basics of qualitative research*, 3rd ed. Thousand Oaks, CA: Sage.

Ethnography

As there are many types of grounded theory, so there are many types of ethnography—but all of these styles of ethnographies have identifying commonalities. All ethnographies are based on some concept of culture, with the assumption that culture is learned, transmitted, and dynamic. This enables the findings of ethnography to be patterned. Culture is considered to be "implicit," that is, those within the culture may not be aware of certain features of their culture, so it is best understood by those from outside, who are not members of the cultural group. And it is this implicitness of culture that makes the findings of ethnographies interesting, exciting, and "new" in what they reveal. Traditionally, ethnographies were conducted in delineated groups ("native communities"), but as ethnography developed in the United States, it moved first to American Indian communities, then to immigrant groups in the cities, to gangs and subgroups within the cities, to institutions (such as schools), to delineated groups within the schools (e.g., classrooms), and to families. Now it is even used with special groups within the community (such as people with spinal cord injuries), even though the participants in the study may not have contact with one another.

Ethnography usually begins with interviews or observations at a very general level, and then, as the researcher's comprehension increases, works toward the collection of more specific data. The first interview questions are generally called "grand tour" questions (Spradley, 1979) ("Tell me. . ."), that give the informant the freedom to describe whatever, as he or she desires. As comprehension increases, insight is gained—often as insight that Agar (1996) calls "rich points." One important characteristic of ethnography is that it consists of three strategies: (1) interviews; (2) participant observation recorded as field notes; and (3) a diary (for the recording of the researcher's subjective, emerging ideas). It may also have an "other"—additional data that may be anything the researcher considers necessary: focus group interviews, photographs, videos, maps, documents, psychometric tests, and so on.

Data are usually analyzed using some type of content analysis (Hsieh & Shannon, 2005), with attention to the linkages between the categories. The completed product may be descriptive or interpretative and may contain some level of theory.

One final note: Ethnography consists of several methodological strategies, but it is usually qualitatively-driven and may even be considered a mixed method in itself, although it is not usually described in those terms.

Resources

Agar, M. (1996). *The professional stranger: An informal introduction to ethnography*. San Diego: Academic Press.

Atkinson, P., Delamont, S., Coffey, A., Lofland, J., & Lofland, L. (2007). *Handbook of ethnography*. Thousand Oaks, CA: Sage.

Phenomenology

Phenomenology is a complete method that may be used as the core method for a qualitatively-driven (QUAL) project. Phenomenology has several major forms. It consists of in-depth interactive interviews (known as phenomenological conversations) that are characterized by their length. It is not uncommon for a phenomenological conversation to extend over several sessions. When conducting these interviews, although the researcher is primarily listening, the conversations are balanced and the researcher may introduce his or her own experience or even use that as a point of reflection. The goal is to reach the meaning or the essence of the phenomenon that is the focus of the study.

Other sources of experiential data may be brought in and used as points of reflection: poetry, biographical and autobiographical writings of others, art, and even movies. A number of strategies are used to increase understanding: tracing etymological sources, searching idiomatic phrases, obtaining experiential descriptions, observing, and reflecting on the phenomenological literature. Phenomenologists use these processes for identifying themes, and reflecting, reading, writing, and re-reflecting (van Manen, 1990).

Resources

Dahlberg, K., Nystrom, M. & Drew, N., (2008). *Reflective lifeworld research,* 2nd ed. Sweden: Studentlitteratur Ab.

Spielberg, H. (1975). *Doing phenomenology. Essays on and in phenomenology.* The Hague, Netherlands: Martinus Nijhoff.

van Manen, M. (1990). *Researching the lived experience: Human science for an action sensitive pedagogy.* London, Ontario, Canada: Althouse Press.

Participant Observation

QUAL mixed method designs may be driven by some level of participant observation, which is used as a method. We write "some level" of participant observation as a method because the amount of involvement between the researchers in the setting changes the nature of the participation from *complete observation* (nonparticipant observation) to complete participation in which the person is completely a part of the group he or she is observing, with various mixes of participation and nonparticipation in-between.

Data are usually recorded as field notes, interspersed between periods of observation. Observations usually begin in an unstructured way and become more targeted as the study progresses. Spradley (1980) developed a matrix checklist, to ensure that observations are comprehensive. The timing of observations may depend on the nature of the setting and the topic. Other forms of data may be added to the participant observation core: interviews, recorded dialogues, photographs as well as documents, maps of the setting, staffing diagrams policies, and memos.

Resources

Angrosino, M. (2007). *Participant observation*. Walnut Creek, CA: Left Coast Press.
Spradley, J. P. (1980). *Participant observation*. New York: Holt, Rinehart & Winston.

Video Ethnography

Videos have both advantages and disadvantages over participant observation as a method, and may, of course, be used as the core method for QUAL mixed method designs. Their main advantage is that when used remotely, the participants quickly forget about the camera, so these video observations have little impact on behavior. With video, transient behaviors are recorded in a permanent form, and may be replayed quickly or slowly, and analyzed globally (from a macro perspective) as well as examined microanalytically.

The major limitation of video ethnography arises from the limitations of filming. Unless the researcher is using a hand-held camera, there is a limited "stage" of action, and many important actions may occur off-camera or at times when the researcher is not filming.

Data may be recorded as field notes (as from observation) or, depending on the research question, segments of film may be identified and coded more microanalytically. Pertinent segments of the film may be copied into separated files (similar to the strategies used in textual content analysis to separate significant sections from the interview itself), so that similar behaviors can be more easily compared. The results of video ethnography are usually presented as a research narrative.

Resources

Bottorff, J. L. (1994). Using videotaped recordings in qualitative research In *Critical issues in qualitative research methods*, J. Morse, ed. (pp. 244–261). Thousand Oaks, CA: Sage.
Stanczak, G. (2007). *Visual research methods*. Thousand Oaks, CA: Sage.

Toward Quantification: The *quan* Supplemental Component

The supplemental components add dimensions to the qualitative core. Simultaneous components measure, describe, compare, document change, and confirm. Sequential components add dimensions that compare, test, identify patterns, determine distributions of the theory in the populations, and allow at least preliminary testing of the emerging theory. Note, however, that some of these functions will not be done definitively in mixed method design (as we have defined it), but rather considered solid indicators. More definitive studies should be done as multiple method design.

Enhancing QUAL with Quantitative Description

The qualitative researcher's reluctance to measure comes from constant admonishment from quantitative researchers that unless they attend to sampling issues, they "will not know anything and cannot make any claims." Even if their measurement is accurate, statements cannot be made about the typicality of such measure because of the untypical nature of their sample. As a result, qualitative researchers cautiously use general terms to designate quantities and usually don't use numbers to describe their phenomenon in concrete terms. This is unfortunate, as much good description is lost.

Enhancing QUAL with Measurement

How do you decide if something can be "enhanced by measurement"? If you measure something, you have a precise descriptor, and if such descriptors assist in the communication of the results, then it is appropriate to use them. Qualitative researchers are often hesitant to count and may even abhor quantifying, because the sampling frame used to select their sample is not representative of the population and quantifying results in loss of meaning. They feel that precise measures will mislead. Yet, they often use less precise "descriptors" such as few, many, more, most, some, and so forth to indicate *approximations of quantity*, and to give the reader some idea of frequency. Using a QUAL-*quan* design enables both qualitative and quantitative perspectives regarding quantification to be respected. QUAL-*quan* designs may use the *quan* components to *enhance QUAL studies with measurement*, providing descriptions or illustration, revealing how much or how many, enabling comparison or confirmation.

QUAL + *quan* Simultaneous Designs

With a qualitative core component (QUAL) and a quantitative supplementary component (*quan*), the qualitative sample (purposefully selected and small) does not meet the quantitative criteria of adequacy (much larger and randomly selected). If the researcher has an adequately large qualitative sample—perhaps because semistructured interviews are being used *and* can "live with" the limitation of using a nonrandom sample—then the researcher may measure the necessary characteristic from qualitative sample directly.

QUAL + *quan* to Measure

Direct Measurement
With simultaneous design, if *direct* measurement of the qualitative sample is used for the quantitative supplementary component data to enhance description (for instance, to measure participant anxiety or obesity), then the quantitative instrument used must have external norms. You are not comparing each person in the sample with each other, but with a large and normative population score. The scores

obtained for the participants in the small qualitative sample may then be interpreted within the distribution of the normative population, so the researcher can draw conclusions about *how obese* the participants in the sample are when compared with the normal population. The quantitative information is then added to the description of the participants in the *results narrative* as the point of interface. The scores obtained from the qualitative participants may not be averaged and presented as group scores, unless the sample size meets the minimum sample size; rather, scores are reported with the description of each participant.

Principle #13: If you can measure, measure. Just keep any limitations in mind.

How "strong" are these results? It depends, of course, on what you are measuring and the importance and the role of these measurements in your results. As we tell our students, these measurements are the "Oh, my!" and the "Fancy that!" of the project—they are things that may be worth exploring more completely in subsequent research, rather than the certainty of more definitive findings.

QUAL + *quan* to Provide Broad Comparisons

A second *direct* technique using the qualitative core data is to sort the qualitative interviews as they are conducted according to some characteristic identified (such as gender or ethnicity) and making comparisons between the groups of interviews. The researcher codes the pertinent characteristic in the qualitative interviews in the core component itself and conducts quantitative analyses separately on each set of data.

Two prerequisites are necessary for coding qualitative characteristics:

1. *Data about the characteristic of interest must be obtained from all participants or must be present in all interviews.* All participants must have gender, age, or ethnicity recorded. Equivalent data are obtained if all of the participants have been asked the same questions in approximately the same order (as in semistructured, open-ended interviews), or if the answers can be inferred from the interviews (e.g., the same five or six guiding questions have been used for all interviews).

   Data cannot be transformed if the researcher has used unstructured interviews that have evolved as the study has progressed, as is often done in ethnography, grounded theory, or phenomenology. In these modes of data collection, participants are asked different questions as the study progresses in search of deeper understanding.

   If, however, in analysis it becomes clear that the same data *are* available from all participants (even if not intentionally collected to ensure this), and necessary responses may be inferred from data, then it may be possible to proceed with quantification and limited nonparametric statistical analysis to make broad comparisons. In certain circumstances, using dichotomous variables (e.g., presence/absence), the interview may be coded from each participant, and these correlated with another dichotomous variable such as gender or marital status. Should a researcher attempt to numerically code such interviews, it will be evident that the percentage of missing data will render any transformation efforts useless. Results must always be interpreted with consideration of the sample size and sampling frame, making tentative conclusions.

2. *There must be an adequate number of participants (or interviews) to conduct the analysis once the interviews have been sorted into sub-groups or categorized.* This means that enough participants must have been interviewed so that when the interviews are split into two or more groups, there are enough to use nonparametric statistics (such as chi square) to conduct the quantitative analysis for comparison.

QUAL + *quan* to Compare

The most basic level of measurement is to determine the presence or absence of a certain characteristic within each unstructured interview. Yet even at this most basic level, the investigator may create hypotheses to test using qualitative textual data.

Again, the necessary condition is that whatever data are being counted is available for all participants. Most obvious, demographic data are useful for researchers' comparisons: interviews obtained from males and females, or the elderly and young participants, or employed with unemployed, or ethnic groups compared with each other, and so forth. These data sorts are easily done if the researcher is using a computer data analysis program—data will re-sort/recategorize automatically (see Bazeley, 2006 and Richards, 2005). However, one must keep in mind that the original sample size must be adequate to obtain saturation in each of the subgroups, even if the subgroups are unevenly distributed.

Direct measurement, therefore, is conducted with simultaneous mixed method design, and the quantitative data are collected at the time that the qualitative interviews are conducted. If direct measurement is not possible (as with a sequential design, when the researcher does not have access to the original qualitative sample), or if the qualitative sampling limitations are too much of a threat to validity, then a *new quantitative sample must be drawn from the study population,* according to the needs of the quantitative measures. The simultaneous QUAL + *quan* research design, and drawing a quantitative sample, is shown on Figure 8.3.

QUAL + *quan* to confirm

Occasionally, the role of the supplemental component is to *confirm* the findings of the core component. Researchers hope for replication or overlap of the findings, as reassurance or as an indicator of validity of the core findings. This was a common reason for conducting

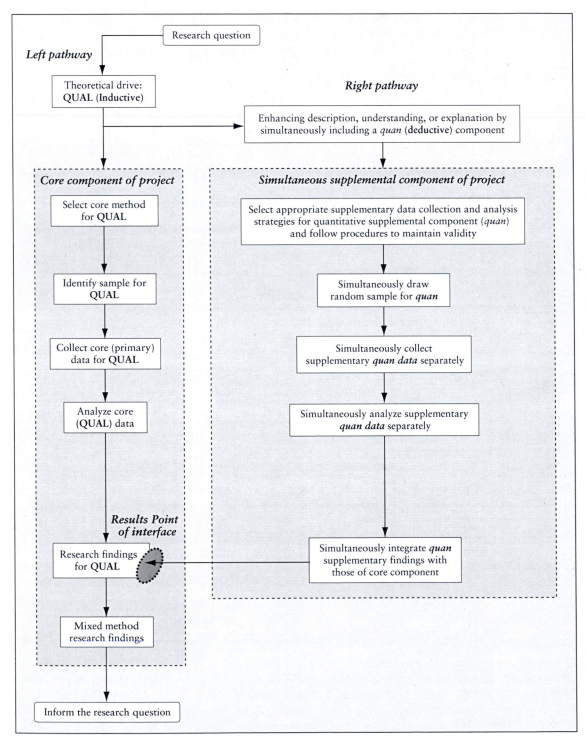

Figure 8.3 QUAL + quan mixed method design, using an external quantitative sample

triangulated studies, but it is less common now that the methods of internal validation during the conduct of qualitative inquiry (Meadows & Morse, 2001) are understood. In fact, the reverse design is true: Researchers are now more likely to conduct a qualitative component to validate the use of a quantitative scale.

When using a mixed method QUAL + *quan* design for confirmation, the most critical issue is to ensure that the quantitative measure is a valid indicator of the concept. The instrument should be well established and well validated in a number of settings.

As shown in Figure 8.3, a separate sample is drawn from the same population from which the qualitative sample was obtained. How large should the sample be? That depends on the type of instrument you are using, and there are established guidelines. For instance, the sample size will depend on the number of items the instrument contains. The sample size will also depend on the stability of whatever you are measuring, or the amount of variation it has in the population. But if the measure is well established, and has been used extensively by other researchers, then the researcher can use it with more confidence and a smaller sample may be used. However, remember that the purpose of doing mixed methods is to not fall into the trap of conducting a multiple method study, but to move on once one is confident enough of the findings.

QUAL—>*quan* Sequential Design

QUAL—>*quan* sequential design is usually dependent on one of two procedures for obtaining data: (1) collecting new data for quantification and comparison; and (2) transforming descriptive data from the QUAL component to quantify (see Boyatzis, 1998). (This is direct sequential design, as the qualitative data are transformed directly to create the mixed method design). In both cases, the analysis does, of course, take place separately from the QUAL analysis, and the point of interface is in the *results narrative*. This means discussing both the qualitative and the quantitative results in the same section, even though the qualitative analysis must wait for publication until the quantitative component has been completed.

QUAL—>QUAN To Measure Change

This is an important design for evaluation studies. If the purpose of the evaluation is to demonstrate changes over time, the measure selected and the timing of the measurement are important and specific to each project. The quantitative measures may be direct (if the researchers has access to the participants) or a new sample is drawn (see Figure 8.4).

If the change occurs as a result of a naturalistic experiment, and the core qualitative method is grounded theory, the study is a little more complex. If the grounded theory is to be done with retrospective interviews (rather than following the person through the experience), and, for instance, the supplemental quantitative component requires

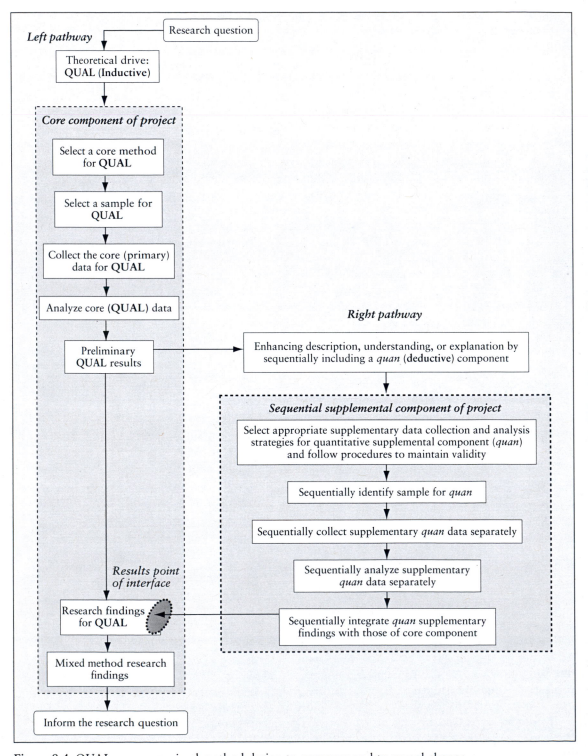

Figure 8.4 QUAL—>quan mixed method design to compare and to reveal change

physiological measures of the core participant, how does one obtain those measures? The researcher's identification of the grounded theory stages and phases may not be completed when the measures are to be collected (i.e., the project cannot be conducted simultaneously).

There are several options:

1. If one is lucky, then the measures will be available from medical records or some other source, for the time frame necessary;

2. If one is unlucky, the measures may have be collected simultaneously, before the grounded theory analysis and interviews have been completed, in which case they would be collected "blindly" regardless of the stages and phases of the grounded theory, and later placed on the theoretical foundation and hopefully fit the emerging model;

3. Or the measures can be collected from a different and new sample according the time frame necessary.

NOTE: There is an important point to make about the second option: Even if the quantitative data are collected BEFORE the QUAL grounded theory is completed, this does NOT make the study a *quan*—>QUAL. The study remains a QUAL—>*quan*. Recall the pacing of the components is not a temporal assignment, but according to conceptual contribution of each component. The QUAL grounded theory provides us with the conceptual information that makes the *quan* measure make sense, and it is not useful until the grounded theory gives us that information.

QUAL—>*quan* to Test Conjectures

If conducted sequentially, the quantitative component may be used to test conjectures arising from the direct analysis of the qualitative core. To do this, a minimum of two variables are needed for comparison, again at the most basic level, the presence or absence of two characteristics, or by coding two variables. This will enable the researchers to conduct a chi square and obtain a p value, *supporting or rejecting* the hypotheses (see Figure 8.5).

For example, Morse (1987) was studying perceptions of health in the inner city. All participants had been asked: "what was health to you?" if you "considered yourself healthy?" and "what do you do to keep healthy?" The first two questions were easily coded: (1) Did the participants describe health in physical or psychological terms? (2) Was self-assessment of health described as a state of the presence of absence of illness? These answers provided data that enabled a 2×2 chi square that could easily be tested, and these results *added to* the textual description. When we examined the interviews for self-descriptions of health status, we noted that those who described themselves as healthy gave a psychological definition of the health (health = happiness), whereas those who rated their own health as

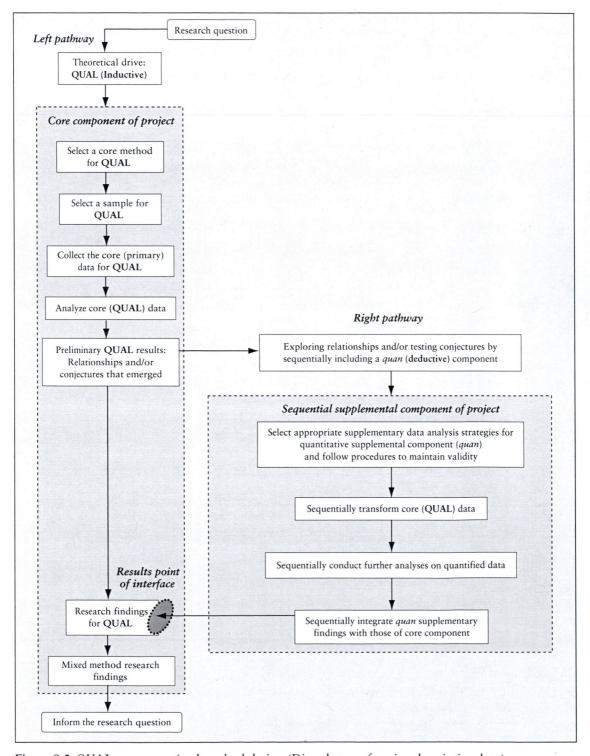

Figure 8.5 QUAL—>quan mixed method design (Directly transforming descriptive data)

poor gave a physiological definition of health (health = pain-free, disease-free), and this relationship was statistically significant.

Admittedly, such measurement is crude, but if the assumptions can be met—it does add an interesting dimension to the inquiry. In this way, mixed method design allows for a more complete understanding than can be obtained by a single method (interviews and content analysis) used alone. However, the combining of a core method with a supplementary strategy, in particular qualitative and quantitative strategies, requires expert understanding of the principles of both qualitative and quantitative methods, and knowledge of sampling strategies and data transformation, to maintain validity.

NOTE: This data analysis strategy is sequential, because the transformation of the qualitative data cannot be performed until the qualitative analysis is completed. BUT this quantitative analysis informs the research findings at the point of interface, rather than building on the results per se.

QUAL—>*quan* to Identify Patterns

Often behaviors are so subtle that although one suspects that behavior is patterned, because it is complex and complicated one cannot determine exactly what those patterns are, or even identify their components. *Human ethology* (Eibl-Eibesfeldt, 1989; Lehner, 1979) enables the identification of these patterns. It consists of qualitative observations of human behaviors that are then quantified as follows:

1. observational description and the preparation of an ethogram (a textual description of all possible behaviors, their antecedents, and their outcomes);

2. development of a code book (i.e., codes and definitions developed for each and every possible movement);

3. coding the movements according to some sampling frame (e.g., continuous coding or the coding whenever a movement changes, or coding by time—in seconds or minutes); and

4. factor analysis of interval-level data to uncover groupings of behaviors that are not obvious.

In human ethology, the sample size is not the number of persons in the study, but the number of measurements. Note we are transforming observations into textual data (to develop codes), then transforming coded observations into numerical values.

An interesting example was an early study by Judy Côté (Côté, Morse, & James, 1991). In the early 1980s, pediatricians believed that infants, having immature nervous systems, did not perceive pain. This belief led to many procedures being done without analgesia—such as circumcision and chest tubes insertion, for example. Côté collected data by videotaping four infants for 12 hours and four post operative infants for 12 hours and coded all of their movements and contextual variables every 5 minutes. The factor analysis uncovered five behavioral states: quiet and alert, drowsy, no distress, subacute distress, and active distress. Observations showed that the first response to pain in the infant was the separation of the large toe from the second toe as the leg extended, followed by a furrowed brow.

We have used ethology in a number of studies—in particular when we are interested in behaviors and the clients are unable to be interviewed. In addition to the infant study (above), we have explored:

- elderly patients with Alzheizmer's communication patterns (Morse & Intrieri, 1997) and the behavioral effects of removing restraints (Morse & McHutchion, 1991);

- subconscious behaviors as in touching during nursing care (Bottorff & Morse, 1994); and

- nurse-comforting infants (Morse, Solberg, & Edwards, 1993; Solberg & Morse, 1991).

The next two designs, contributing to the generalizability of the qualitative core, may be conducted as a mixed method design and the results published as one publication, or they may be conducted as two interrelated, but complete projects, as a multiple method project. This decision depends, in part, on the certainty and the completeness of the quantitative component.

Example: Côté, J. J., Morse, J. M., & James, S. G. (1991). The pain experience of the post-operative newborn. *Journal of Advanced Nursing, 16,* 378–387.

Design	Theoretical drive: Inductive	Pacing: Sequential
	QUAL component: Observation	*quan* component: data transformation
	Point of Interface: Analysis	

QUAL—>*quan* to determine the distribution in the population

The most common design to determine how the qualitative findings are distributed in a population is to follow the qualitative core component with a quantitative survey. The survey is constructed directly from the core qualitative results, with the items reflecting both the qualitative categories and the language of the participants.

The instrument should be developed according to standard procedures, pretested to ensure the items are "good," and ordered logically for the respondents (Bradburn, Sudman, & Wansink, 2004). Consideration must also be given to the sampling frame and the sample size. The analysis may be presented as frequencies or, with adequate sampling, even multivariate analysis.

In this QUAL—>*quan* study, Palestinian children's political socialization were examined. First, focus groups and interviews were conducted with children and analyzed. It is not clear from the analysis if the researchers analyzed these two data sets together or separately. However, the quantitative instrument was developed from them. This instrument, initially with 158 items, was submitted to children 9–14 years at 30 schools.

The most interesting thing about this study is that following the presentation of the results from the administration of the scale, the authors *then* present the qualitative findings. Note that although the presentations of the findings are not synchronized with the actual conduct of the study, this does not alter the sequential nature of the design.

Example: QUAL—>*quan* for Instrument Development
Habashi, J., & Worley, J. (2009). Child geopolitical agency: A mixed methods case study. *Journal of Mixed Methods, 3*(1), 42–64.

Design	Theoretical drive: Inductive	Pacing: Sequential
	QUAL component: Focus groups and interviews	*quan* component: instrument
	Point of Interface: Analysis	

QUAL—>*quan* to Test Emerging Theory

Qualitative researchers who have the agenda of developing theory usually diagram their theory, have well-developed constructs, and have adequate description about the linkages between the constructs, so that the theory is amenable to quantitative testing. The testing may take the form of reconstructing/replicating the structure of the concepts as a test of validation, using some form of factor/cluster analysis. Alternatively, the researcher may use some form of modeling to test the linkages between the qualitatively derived concepts.

A Last Word about QUAL-*quan*

Finally, in QUAL-*quan* designs, the most important principle is: *What is being coded and counted must make sense,* and validity may be threatened by *in*appropriate quantification (Sandelowski, 2000, 2003). Certain features of the qualitative data should not be tabulated, including the frequency of words, sentence length, and, when the qualitative sample has been purposefully selected, the percentage of participants who identify a particular theme (Onwuegbuzie & Teddlie, 2003) or comprise a category that is meaningless (i.e., does not contribute to the findings). Similarly, the descriptive "profiling" (Sandelowski, 2001) or "coding" (Richards & Morse, 2007) of a qualitative sample is not quantitative data transformation (i.e., "quantitizing") (Tashakkori & Teddlie, 1998). Describing a sample in frequencies and percentages does not alter the nature of the data collected or the analysis, and again, because of the lack of randomization of the sample, does not add to the interpretation of data.

QUAL-*qual* Designs

For the qualitative researcher, QUAL-*qual* designs should be the easiest to conduct. The core project (QUAL) may be grounded theory, ethnography, phenomenology, participant observation, or even semistructured interviews, and the supplemental (*qual*) component may be required to expand the perspective of the core component. The *qual* sample of the core project would, for a QUAL-*qual* project not be inadequate, but the issue is, would it be appropriate? Would the participants for the core project be able to provide the information required for the supplemental project, and have they already done so (i.e., is the information already to be found in the interviews?).

For example, if you have unstructured qualitative interviews for the core project, and have conducted a grounded theory from these, if you then decide to add a supplemental component, can you use the same data twice?

It *is* possible to use some of the data that were gathered for the core project for the supplemental project, but with a caveat. When you are conducting qualitative research using a particular method, the data are in the form that best suits the method that you were intending to use. For example, if you are doing grounded theory, unstructured retrospective interviews make the identification of the grounded theory process easier than if you were collecting data longitudinally and interviewing participants as you went along. The form of data for the grounded theory is not necessarily well suited to use for a second study, especially if the information necessary is not in the data! You will need to collect additional data. If you do decide to use *some* of the core data for your supplementary project, Thorne (1994) notes that with the secondary use of data you should at least collect some new data to be used for this project alone.

There are two conditions in which a QUAL-*qual* design is appropriate:

1. *To obtain two different perspectives on the same phenomena*: These two perspectives may have some overlap, but most probably will give different information and a different slant on the topic. Therefore, using the same data may mean that these two methods will have greater overlap on the phenomena than may be intended or desired by the researcher.

2. *To obtain data different levels of analysis*: In this case, you may be forced to collect new data. For example, if the supplementary

component consists of some microanalysis of movement, video ethnography, or participant observation, of course you cannot solely use the interview data for this component. However, exploring a phenomenon at different levels, and from different perspectives using different methods, can make the research extremely exciting.

The relationship of QUAL-*qual* components is shown on Figure 8.6. Why do a QUAL-*qual* study? Qualitative inquiry boasts about its holistic qualities, so why would we ever have to use more than one method?

Qualitative methods have a philosophical base and assumptions, and it is this foundation that gives qualitative methods their particular perspective. Therefore, each qualitative method has particular questions that it may answer *better* than other qualitative methods. For instance, grounded theory is masterful at describing change; phenomenology does it very poorly. Phenomenology is excellent for eliciting meaning; ethnography reveals what is going on in a cultural context, and does not do change very well. Grounded theory is good at emotions, ethnography at behavioral patterns, and so forth. The second reason for using qualitative mixed methods is that each method works at a particular "level of analysis." For instance, grounded theory and phenomenology may work with reported conversations: "He told me that . . ." rather then the actual dialogue, which could be microanalyzed using conversational analysis. Participant observation records observations as field notes, but the study of touch, for instance, in which behaviors are transient, must be microanalyzed from videotapes. Thus, often more than one qualitative method is necessary to capture some phenomena.

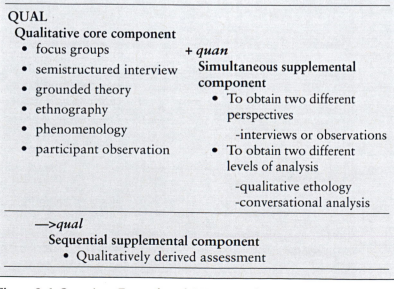

Figure 8.6 Overview: Examples of QUAL-*qual* components

QUAL-*qual* design, with the collection of new data, has the same patterned flow charts for QUAL-*quan* (Figures 8.4 and 8.5), with the supplementary *quan* components replaced with supplementary *qual*. Note that the simultaneous supplementary component is separate from the core component, usually using separate data, because of the different form of the interview data required for different methods, and possibly also because of a slightly different focus for the interview topic. For instance, if the core component is grounded theory, the interviews will be participants' stories from "then to now," according to the topic. Then, if the supplemental component consists perhaps of phenomenological interviews about a specific point in time in the trajectory, these phenomenological conversational interviews will be more in depth than the grounded theory interviews. The participants may or may not be the same people, depending on the information that is required for the supplemental project. Similarly, with sequential QUAL—>*qual* design, with a qualitative core and a qualitative sequential project, the supplemental sample usually consists of different participants than those who participated in the core component. Again, because the researcher is using a different qualitative approach to elicit a different perspective, a different interview and analytic strategies will be used. For both the simultaneous and the sequential mixed method design, the point of interface is in the results narrative.

Purposes of the Supplemental *qual* Components

1. *Creating concepts: Identifying unique data from unstructured interviews.*

    Imagine that you are conducting a phenomenological study and interesting findings emerge in the course of phenomenological interviews that may perhaps warrant further observations. You, the researcher, may decide to "go and see" what is happening and add an observational component.

    Example: In the course of developing research about the use of empathy in the emergency room, we discovered an interesting phenomenon (and had some phenomenological data left over) regarding the concept that we later called *compathy* (Morse & Mitcham, 1997; Morse, Mitcham, & van der Steen, 1998). Although empathy explained the sharing of emotions (and was defined as such), we had data that addressed the sharing of physical pain.

    We used a variety of data sources to develop our understanding of compathy, then this developed into a full-fledged independent study in itself; we were interested in *seeing* the pain responses that were reflected in others. We collected newspaper articles of crowds gathered around accidents, and, rather than focusing on the person who was injured on the ground, we focused on the crowd: Did their faces also reveal expressions of pain? Sometimes expressions of horror were evident. But sometimes their expressions could only be labeled as *pain.* Observers often placed their hands over their mouths, or crossed their arms over themselves, holding the opposite upper arm, as if to self-comfort. Often they clasped the same body part as the injured person. It is from these observations that we developed the preliminary conceptualizations of compathy. We identified examples of the compathetic response in the literature, as in couvade (or the sharing of labor pains) and in the literature of medical students reading about diseases or in the anatomy laboratory. We searched the use of compathy in aversion therapy, as when, for instance, one is shown films of accidents to improve road safety. These sources of *qual* data supplemented the core of QUAL unstructured interviews until a conceptualization of the concept was developed (see Morse & Mitcham, 1997; Morse, Mitcham, & van der Steen, 1998).

2. *Creating studies at different levels of analysis.*

   This type of QUAL + *qual* is similar to building supporting documentation for creating concepts (above) except that different perspectives are deliberately sought. Rather than analyzing two data sets at the same level of abstraction, the second data set may be microanalytic. For instance, we used videos of nurses comforting infants, and the first data set included descriptions of the types of touch, and the effect of that touch on the infant. Next, we conducted microanalysis, analyzing touch frame-by-frame, examining sequence and response. Did nurses touch the infants at the same time the pain appeared? Or did the nurses see the infants grimace and other pain responses and *then* respond by comforting the infant? Macroanalysis is very important for the kind of questions we are asking, but it was the microanalysis of sequence that contributed most to our understanding (see Solberg & Morse, 1991).

   When one has developed a concept from unstructured interviews, the attributes or characteristics are clear within the concept itself. If we are studying hope, we know, for instance, what hope *is,* but the study appears to be only half over, for we do not know how to intervene, how to assess stages of hope, or how to manipulate hope. To get to this level of inquiry, we must continue the study and develop the attribute further to develop an assessment guide.

3. *Creating a qualitatively derived assessment guide.*

   You can make your grounded theory applied by transforming the attributes within the concept from observed behaviors to a question asking if the clinician sees these behaviors as present or absent, enables one to build a reliable and valid assessment guide that identifies the behavioral indices associated with each stage. For example, you may determine at which stage of hope a person may struggle with at a particular behavior. These behaviors may be sequenced and used as indicators for each stage identified. Once the behavioral indicators of the stages of hope that may be assessed are observed, you can then develop assessment questions to identify interventions that will facilitate or modify the development of hope. In this way, the qualitatively derived theory may be made clinically useful (see Morse, Hutchinson, & Penrod, 1998).

4. *Conducting qualitative evaluation*, such as using *Qualitative Outcome analysis (QOA)* (Morse & Penrod, 2000).

   Once an assessment guide is developed, identifying interventions is the next logical step. For instance, it is possible to facilitate the development and maintenance of hope in a particular population, such as spinal cord injured patients. Having done this, it would be necessary to develop a qualitative means to evaluate the analysis. Usually, this is done by adding a supplemental component of observations or interviews to evaluate the project. Did the assessment guide and the interventions elicit the desired changes? (see Penrod & Morse, 1997).

Writing up QUAL-*quan* Designs

For readers and reviewers to be able to trace the development of your article, the results of the QUAL component must be comprehensive and detailed. This presentation must follow normal qualitative conventions, including a discussion of the sample, detailed description of the categories or themes (supported by participants quotes), and development of the concepts and theories. In the next section, present the data obtained from the supplemental core, again starting with the sample and how it was obtained. If the supplemental project was a quantitative project, present these data quantitatively with tables or graphs or whatever is appropriate.

Now develop a third section for presentation of your synthesized results. Importantly, the emerging QUAL model or theory form the theoretical foundation into which the quantitative results fit, expand, or explain (see Greene, 2007; Sandelowski, Voils, & Barroso, 2006). This narrative must be logical, tight, and, from the perspective of the two preceding sections, appear as a logical summary statement. This statement is should be the culmination of your study—the climax of your work!

This is then followed by the Discussion section. In it, you link your findings to the literature and discuss the strengths and weakness of your project, its implications and application(s).

The Qualitatively-Driven Last Word

From the preceding chapter, a very important and often misunderstood point is: The QUAL core provided the theoretical foundations for the supplemental component, and therefore ALWAYS provides the theoretical drive for the project. Make certain you do excellent work with this component, as the quality of the entire study rests on it. The "Always" means that the supplemental cannot logically precede the CORE component—the notation qual—>QUAN simply cannot be good science!

9

Quantitatively-Driven Mixed Method Designs

QUAN, that is, quantitatively-driven mixed method designs—are the most common of the mixed method designs and much easier to do than QUAL mixed methods designs. The QUAN sample is already adequate—usually too large—for the qualitative supplement, and all the researcher has to do is to decide who to choose from the line up for the *qual* sample according to some selected criteria—which sometimes is not easy. As we say: "Certainly not random; convenience is not the best either."

It is simple these days to convince grant review boards that the study will be stronger if a qualitative component is added (for convincing quantitative colleagues that validity will be enhanced is something that qualitative researchers have done well), but exactly what should be added, and how, are still questions worthy of consideration.

What a QUAN-qual is NOT: First, we reiterate *what* a quantitatively-driven mixed method project is *not*. Doing a pilot project before the main study to test your instruments, to test your tool, or just to test the waters to see if you can get a sample does NOT make a mixed method project. Pilot projects may be considered a component separate from the main study, but even if you use a different methodological strategy, because those projects do not contribute conceptually to the overall study, adding a pilot does not make a study mixed method.

Second, it is not a mixed method study if your supplemental component is "complete"—that is, if it is rigorous enough to stand alone and to be published separately. Supplemental components only make sense in conjunction with the core project. Without it, not only are they thin, weak, and poor evidence—they may also not make a lot a sense. If you have a supplemental project that is strong enough to stand alone and be published separately, you are probably doing a multiple method project.

For your review let's look at the QUAN-*qual* mixed method design again (Figure 9.1). There are two alternative routes for the supplemental mixed method design: (1) Simultaneously collect new qualitative data (with the *n* equivalent to the QUAN *sample size*—for instance,

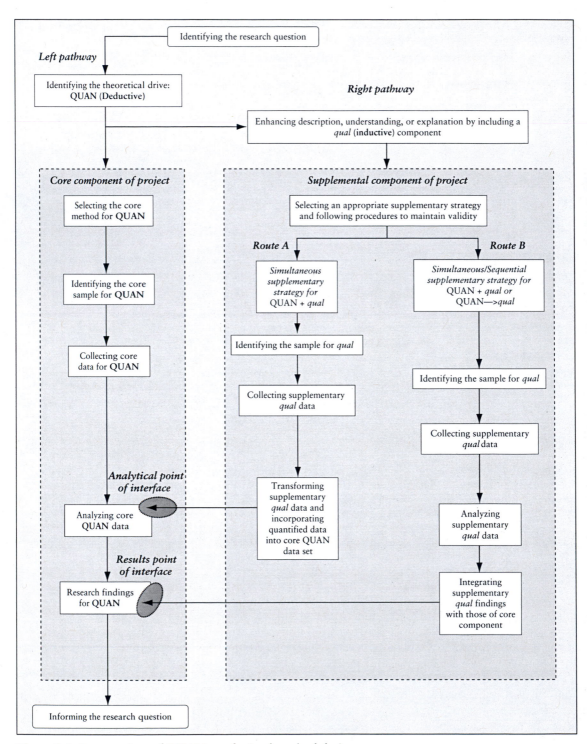

Figure 9.1 An overview of QUAN-*qual* mixed method designs

as semistructured questions), code and transpose these data, and move them into the QUAN data set for analysis (Route A); (2) simultaneously or sequentially collect new *qual* data, analyze these data, and move them into the results narrative with the QUAN findings (Route B).

The Role of the Theoretical Drive

The theoretical drive for quantitatively-driven mixed method design is deductive, and the overall thinking about the project is deductive, regardless of the minor supplemental qualitative components. The QUAN theoretical drive is developed using a theoretical framework and often even with hypotheses for testing. Often, the researcher may be confident enough and knowledgeable enough about a community to conduct a quantitative survey. Quantitatively-driven mixed method research designs may even use experimental designs with an intervention as the core component, to determine group differences.

When using quantitative theoretical drive with a qualitative supplementary component, the qualitative component must fit into the quantitative core in relation to its implementation and point of interface. Between these two points, however, the researcher works *inductively* according to the paradigmatic assumptions of qualitative inquiry (see Figure 9.1, Routes A and B).

The Theoretical Framework

The purpose of the theoretical framework (and under this heading we also include the underlying theory) is to organize the variables and hypothesized relationships between the variables. Through the theoretical framework, the researcher can visualize all aspects of the project, and the ways in which each variable will be measured and will interrelate.

Always begin diagramming your study at this point. Diagramming assists with the conceptualization of each component, their purpose, interrelationship, and pacing.

> Diagram your study design.

Sampling

The core QUAN sample is determined by the requirements of the core QUAN method and the principles of quantitative inquiry. Usually this is predetermined by a power test, by some rule of thumb for numbers of cases necessary per variable or item, or some percentage of the total sample. The sampling selection is based on principles of randomization, so that the sample is representative of the total population.

In QUAN-*qual* design, when the QUAN and the *qual* sample are to use the same people, problems occur because of the different assumptions required for the selection of each sample. Randomization, necessary for quantification, weakens and may even invalidate the qualitative sample and, the QUAN sample size is unmanageable for

> A random sample may invalidate your *qual* component.

most qualitative methods. Therefore, the first question the researchers should ask is:

Is it important that both the QUAN and the *qual* samples consist of the same people?

- If the answer is *no*, then the solution is to draw a separate sample for the *qual* supplemental component, according to the principles of qualitative inquiry.
- If the answer is *yes*, and the QUAN sample IS a feasible size for the *qual* supplemental component, and the *qual* strategy allows for data to be collected from each participant without the researcher collapsing from exhaustion, then the entire sample may be used for the qualitative component.
- If the answer is *yes*, but the QUAN sample consists of a number that makes the *qual* sample not feasible, then some compromise must be reached. The researcher will have to change the *qual* supplemental method to a more efficient method, such as moving from a guided interview to a semistructured interview, a strategy that allows for the data to be coded more effectively.

Pacing

As the quantitative component often takes less time than the qualitative component (i.e., it is conducted more quickly than qualitative inquiry), sometimes the QUAN component has to "wait" for the *qual* analysis to be completed.

Point of Interface

The point of interface for QUAN-*qual* designs is usually the *results narrative*. Only one design allows for the *qual* component data to be moved to the analysis—that is, using semistructured interviews to collect data, including semistructured open-ended questions in a survey. This can occur only when the same sample is used for both the QUAN and the *qual* components and when all of the *qual* sample are asked the same interview questions. Semistructured interviews are the only type of qualitative interview in which the same questions are asked of all participants; these are commonly used in mixed method designs. From these interviews, responses may be coded and transformed into variables and moved into the quantitative data set for analysis. We will write about this strategy later in the chapter.

QUAN: Quantitatively-Driven Core Projects

The Quantitative Core, QUAN

The quantitative component (QUAN) drives the project. This may consist of surveys, standardized questionnaires, or other forms of measurement or even be an experimental design (see Figure 9.2). Each will be discussed below.

Surveys

Surveys are usually designed by the researchers according to the needs of the research questions and are administered within a delimited geographical area or population. Survey questions are usually designed according to the theoretical framework and to elicit the information that is needed.

Questions are designed so that they are easy for the participants to answer; they should be asked in logical order and be clear and unambiguous. Once the questionnaire is designed, researchers will pretest the instrument by administering it to a small group to ensure that the questions are eliciting the intended responses and will be useful. When pretesting the quantitatively-driven mixed method design or pilot work is being conducted, the pilot work is considered a part of the quantitative research design and not a separate component. That is, we will NOT create a design that is *quan—>*QUAN indicating a pilot was done first. This study remains simply a QUAN design.

Resources

Rea, L. M., & Parker, R. A. (2005). *Designing and conducting survey research: A comprehensive guide,* 3rd ed. San Francisco: Jossey-Bass.

Fowler, F. J. (2009). *Survey research methods.* (Applied Social Research Methods Series). Thousand Oaks, CA: Sage.

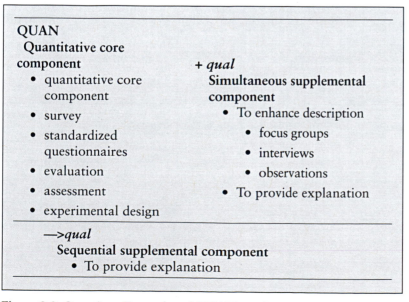

QUAN
  Quantitative core component
  + *qual*
  • quantitative core component
  Simultaneous supplemental component
  • survey
    • To enhance description
  • standardized questionnaires
    • focus groups
    • interviews
  • evaluation
    • observations
  • assessment
    • To provide explanation
  • experimental design

  —>*qual*
    Sequential supplemental component
      • To provide explanation

Figure 9.2 Overview: Examples of QUAN-*qual* components

Standardized Questionnaires

Standardized questionnaires are commonly used strategies for the QUAN core project. Researchers identify the questionnaire that best measures the necessary variables (or best addresses the research question and will be suitable for administration to the identified sample). Researchers then evaluate the reliability and validity of the questionnaire to make certain that it will be adequate. Again, the questionnaire may be pretested with the population to make sure that the questions are appropriate and are providing the kind of information that will be required. And again, the sample size will be determined by the number of variables or items that are being asked in the scale.

Resources

Booth, W. C., Williams, J.M. & Colomb, G., C. (2003). *The craft of research*, 2nd ed. Chicago: University of Chicago Press.

Bradburn, N., Sudman S., & Wansink, B. (2004). *Asking questions: The definitive guide to questionnaire design—For market research, political polls, and social and health questionnaires*. San Francisco: John Wiley & Son.

Supplementary Component for the QUAN-*qual* Design

Purposes of the Supplementary Component

The *qual* supplemental component of the QUAN projects is intended to compensate for the inadequacies in meaning or detail that occurs with the quantitative core. The qualitative strategy allows the researcher to "connect the dots" between variables or concepts or link the quantitative research to the context or to the applied knowledge required for the clinical setting. The qualitative methods allow the researcher to explain, ground the concepts, link variables, or interpret findings.

Description to Explain

Quantitative research is often abstract and decontextualized, and while it is this strength that enables measurement, it is also its weakness. Often, in the Discussion section, the researcher will explain the implications of the project. Although he or she may quantitatively explain the social economic status or employment/nonemployment of those who use the setting, qualitative description of contextual details about the setting provides a much richer explanation of conditions under which the study was conducted.

Description to Ground

"Grounding" is the linking of the results with the setting, so the findings may be applied. Often it is not immediately obvious how quantitative research may be implemented into a setting and what relevance it has. A strong QUAN—>*qual* design would enable the findings to be maximally useful when published. Qualitative strategies, such as participant observation techniques or unstructured interviews within the context, allows the reader to understand exactly what the limitations and relevance a particular study has in a setting. Note that in the example below, all the information about treatment is presented as a case study.

The quantitatively-driven study sequential mixed method design is described by the authors as a "clinic-based ethnography." From the literature, they present an extensive description of the Vietnamese migration to the United States and trauma-related disorder in the "cross-cultural perspective," including the model of orthostatic panic attacks (pp. 81–92).

Participants were administered four interviews/scales measuring: (1) orthostatic panic symptoms and, if present, its (2) severity, (3) incidence in the past month, and (4) degree of dissociation experienced every visit to the clinic. Data for this study were taken from 85 patient charts in month prior to 9/11 and one month after, and the scores for the two data points were compared.

The sequential qualitative component consisted of interviews with 10 patients. These patients were shown the orthostatic panic model, its causation and asked if "that explanation matched his or her understanding" (p. 93). Treatments were then based on this model: "Trauma associations were discussed, and new, empowering imagery was associated to dizziness" (p. 95). The point of interface of the two components is in the Results section, with the results of each components presented in separate sections. To illustrate the experience of the Vietnamese in their article, the authors present one detailed case study (pp. 95–99). The authors conclude that the collapse of the Twin Towers in New York City had a symbolic meaning of "great emotional significance" for the Vietnamese, and attending to orthostatic panic in assessment leads to more culturally sensitive and effective care.

Example: QUAN—>*qual*

Hinton, D. E., Nguyen, L., & Pollack, M.H. (2007). Orthostatic panic events as a key Vietnamese reaction to traumatic events: The case of September 11, 2001. *Medical Anthropological Quarterly, 21*(1), 81–107.

Design	Theoretical drive: Deductive Pacing: Sequential
	QUAN component: 4 instru- *qual* component: interviews ments
	Point of Interface: Results

Description to Link

While in a quantitative research framework, a researcher may have created linkages between particular concepts that are being measured.

In fact, when it comes to writing up the research, the researcher may still be uncomfortable about the linkages between the individual concepts that have been measured and the core component. Again, unstructured interviews with participants will enable the researcher to build conceptual bridges between these concepts, justify their inclusion, and, using qualitative data, link each concept in the context. These linkages will make the resulting study more useful, more relevant, and easier to build subsequent studies on.

Description to Interpret

A quantitative study may, at the time of analysis, produce surprises or findings that are not expected. Often it is these findings that are most frequently used and are most significant. In the example below, the interpretation is to explore a longstanding puzzle of continued treatment to people whose back pain is not improving.

The purpose of the survey was to determine how widespread long-term treatment without improvement was for people with low back pain and to interview practitioners about their beliefs for continuing treatment. Three hundred fifty-four clinicians responded (54%), with at least 10% stating that the continued treatment. Fourteen clinicians from each of the three professions (chiropractors, osteopaths, and physiotherapists) were interviewed. Clinicians considered their role expanded to counseling and health education, rather the "cure or refer." In addition, there was no referral pathway, so that ceasing treatment meant a "therapeutic void." In this study, the researchers have presented the quantitative and the qualitative results separately in the results section, but have integrated them seamlessly in the discussion.

Example:
Pincus, Y., Vogel, S., Breen, A., Foster, N., & Underwood, M. (2005). Persistent back pain—Why do physical therapy clinicians continue treatment? A mixed methods study of chiropractors, osteopaths and physiotherapists. *European Journal of Pain, 10,* 67–76.

Design	Theoretical drive: Deductive QUAN component: Survey Point of Interface: Results	Pacing: Sequential *qual* component: Semistructured interviews

---

QUAN—>*qual* Component Increasing Understanding

Enhancing QUAN with Meaning

The *qual* component, as an incomplete method, consists of strategies of various types of interviews that are continued until the researcher is certain about the necessary information, rather than having obtained enough data to ensure saturation (as is necessary with a complete method). Those interviews most commonly used are unstructured interviews, semistructured interviews, or focus groups and are analyzed by content analysis or by identifying themes.

Unstructured Interviews

These interviews usually consist of a "grand tour" question. Participants are invited to tell their story, or several (perhaps up to six) guiding questions that give them with a relative amount of freedom to provide the information that is necessary within a broad framework, without the researcher overly controlling the interview. By an "open-ended unstructured interview," we do not mean an open-ended question placed at the end of the questionnaire. The information that is obtained from an unstructured interview is in depth; it allows for a narrative to be told at the participant's own pace, and is targeted at a broader issue than those that are placed at the end of a questionnaire.

When conducting an open-ended unstructured interview, the researcher invites the participant to "tell me." Questions may be:

"Tell me about your illness?" or
"Tell me what it is like to have a heart attack?" or
"Tell me what it is like to live with a hyperactive child?"

The operative words are "Tell me. . . ." The researcher assumes a listening stance, and the participant, in telling, becomes immersed in the story. These participants may begin their story hesitantly by providing contextual data that contains demographic data, a who's who of the family or the work place, or whatever the interview is about, and then they begin to build their story. In the third stage, participants become immersed in their story—they may cry, provide details about the meaning of the event, and so forth. In the last stage, they bring the interview to the present time—often to closure—and may end the interview talking to the interviewer about trivial events, laughing, and generally expressing relief (Corbin & Morse, 2003).

The researcher does not interrupt the participant while he or she is telling the story, unless the story becomes confusing. Rather, the researcher stacks questions at the back of his or her mind to be asked at the end of the narrative. Usually these interviews have one common strand or story-line, and the interviewer will follow that strand. For instance, the participant may say, ". . . and my brother went off and joined the navy while I, . . ." and they continue with their own story. At the end of the interview the researcher may say, "You said your brother went off to the navy—where is he now?" and, if it is relevant, you then obtain the story of the brother.

These interviews generally provide a distinct theme that the participants assume that the researcher wants to know. For example, if we are interviewing a person about their illness and the person tells us their "medical" story (which is often little more than a listing of their symptoms, their surgeries, their pills, and their visit to the doctor), at the end of the story the researcher may ask the person to revisit the beginning by asking, "You have told me about your treatments, now I want to know how you feel about your illness." And then listen to the *person's* story. However, in our experience, usually the participant integrates such technical or their personal details and provides an interview that contains both of these elements. Open-ended unstructured interviews are then analyzed either by identifying themes or using content analysis.

Textual Analysis by Developing Themes

Analyzing a narrative for themes is always question driven. The researcher will be exploring the text, reflecting on the content, and using the following techniques:

1. Read the entire text through. Reflect on "what the text is about," its main message or overall message and sub-messages. Then revisit your research question and revise the research question accordingly.

2. Now examine the text line by line, paragraph by paragraph, or even word by word. Highlight significant portions of the text (this may, of course, be done on the computer).

3. Go through the text again carefully and slowly. Make notes by inserting these notes directly into the text using upper-case letters to differentiate it from the person's transcription.

4. On the last pass through the text, again examine the text line by line, word by word, or paragraph by paragraph, asking your research question of that particular section of text. Using the footnote feature of your computer, make footnotes for every significant piece of text. In the footnote, copy your upper-case notes or write a further summary about what the text means, implies, infers, or suggests.

5. Once that is completed—and this is the trick—using your software program, *change* the footnotes to endnotes. Now you have a detailed summary of your notes about the text. Read and reflect on these notes very carefully. You can even make this piece of text the main document and continue making footnotes and further interpretations and insights. It is this process that will enable you to develop your themes. From these notes you may see that you have identified notes about one theme, two themes, or more. Sort these notes accordingly, and synthesize your comments.

How are these themes then incorporated into the results? In a quan-core project, the quantitative findings form the base of the analysis. In the narrative of the text, the researcher may then add detail from the information or the descriptions obtained from the themes. We will discuss this later in the chapter.

Textual Analysis by Content Analysis

When analyzing text using content analysis, the researcher begins to perceive in much the way one does when developing themes. The researcher first reads the interview through carefully and then rereads the interview, coding words and phrases by highlighting the text using italics, bold, colors, or changing the font on the word-processing package. Next (and here the two methods differ), the researcher goes through the interview very carefully and separates out the significant parts of the interview by copying those phrases into a number of files. Content that is about the same topic goes into the same file along with the interviewer's participant number and page number where the section was removed. Each piece of text is separated by a line from other pieces of text, but one copies into this file or highlights any notes that have been made from that particular piece of text.

Once the researcher has copied a number of pieces of text, these categories are ready for further analysis. If the categories are exceedingly long, they may be further subdivided into several categories.

Semistructured Questionnaires

Semistructured interviews are the most common qualitative strategy used in mixed method design (Bryman, 2006b, 2008). Again, the researcher may have a topic or area about which he or she cannot anticipate all the answers but does know all the questions. The researcher lists possible open-ended question stems and places them in an order that makes sense for the participant to answer logically. The person administrating the semistructured questionnaire is free, once the participant has begun his or her answer, to use probes or to ask for further information. Sometimes these probes or requests for additional information are written as prompts in with the question stem. The researcher must pretest his questionnaires to make sure that the question stem is eliciting the correct response from the participants.

Data are analyzed all at once, following the collection of all of the data. Prepare data for analysis by transcribing of all respondents answers to each question into separate files. For instance, all of the answers to question 1 are listed by subject number, then all of the answers to question 2 are listed by subject number, and so forth. Although these semistructured questionnaires may be analyzed using content analysis, kept and further analyzed as textual data, they may also be transformed into numerical data and incorporated into the data set at the data analysis point of interface.

Open-Ended Questions

The most common way that qualitative research contributes to quantitatively-driven research is by inserting open-ended questions within a qualitative survey or questionnaire. When the researcher is certain about the domain of inquiry (i.e., knows about all the areas that should be included in the questionnaire and can draw boundaries around the topic) and can create questions to address all of these areas, but cannot predetermine the answers for some questions, then those questions are managed qualitatively. Usually this is done in the form of a question stem followed by a number of lines, and the person filling out the questionnaire is permitted to write freely.

There are not many rules for writing these questions. The questions or items are usually in the form of the beginning of a sentence (called the question stem), followed by a colon. The interviewer pauses at this point, and the participant then adds his or her own thoughts and opinions. The question stem may or may not be a question (see Chapter 8 for examples of semistructured questions).

These responses are then transcribed verbatim, and once the researcher receives all the responses back, they are copied into a computer file, item by item. Thus, one file will hold all of the responses to question 1, another to question 2, labeled by participant number. The researcher then codes these responses following a form of content analysis. All of the response that are similar are placed in the same category, definitions are developed for the categories, and interrater reliability is obtained (Burla et al., 2008). Once a reasonable level of reliability is obtained, the researcher codes all of these responses numerically and moves these numbers into the quantitative data set as a variable or variables.

Thus, using unstructured questions within a survey enables the researcher to increase the validity of the questionnaire because the questionnaire, with the use of transposed textual descriptive responses, now covers the topic more comprehensively.

Problems occur when a large proportion of the respondents skip over and do not answer the unstructured questionnaires. Too much missing data renders the item useless.

An Open-Ended Unstructured Interview

Open-ended, unstructured interviews exist in a number of styles, under various names. Although there are some differences between these interviews, all have important common characteristics:

- All provide the participants a large degree of freedom to tell their story in the form and style of their own choosing, to provide an account of their own experience, and the events that occurred from their own perspective. The control of the interaction is with the participant.
- The interviewer assumes the role of listener, rather than the interrogator.
- The interviews are conducted in an atmosphere of trust and intimacy.

These interviews come under a variety of labels: unstructured interviews, conversational interviews, interactive interviews, and so forth. They are NOT in the form of an interview that we see on late-night

television, in which the interviewer is playing an active (and sometimes amusing) role, edging on the interviewee; nor are they open-
ended questions at the end of the questionnaire.

In these interviews, the researcher's role is one of passive listening.
The researcher may start the interview with a broad question, "Tell
me . . ." and then absorb the participant's story. The researcher will
not interrupt the participant, unless he or she becomes confused and
needs to clarify what is going on. If it is necessary to interrupt, then
it hardly matters, for the participants becomes so engrossed in their
own narrative that, when interrupted, they will just pick up where
they left off.

The participants will begin their story *tentatively*, providing background, demographic, and contextual information. Next, the participant becomes involved in his or her story, in the *immersion phase*.
Participants may become emotional, even cry, with the researcher
maintaining an empathetic silence. As the participant's story is drawing to a close, the phase of *emergence* is reached, with the participant
returning to the present time (Corbin & Morse, 2003). The research
often needs to debrief the participants and provide tea and cookies
before ending the session.

Other types of unstructured interview allow for more of a balanced
interaction between the researcher and the participant. Conversational
interviews as used in phenomenology, for instance, allow the researcher
to share his or her own experiences.

Guided Interviews

When conducting guided interviews, the researcher prepares six or
more unstructured questions, which are asked of everyone. These
questions form a broad framework for all interviews, and therefore
ensure that the interviews follow a certain form and all contain particular necessary information. These interviews are more controlled by
the researcher than unstructured interviews.

How many unstructured interviews are conducted when used in the
supplementary component? The answer is: as many as it takes to get
the necessary information and the required degree of certainty. This
is probably fewer interviews than would be required if completing a
formal project—researchers do not saturate their findings, but neither
are they careless and sloppy in their work. The number of interviews
conducted also depends on the type of information they are gather-
ing: Is it concrete information or inferential? Is it simple or complex?
Is there a lot of agreement or disagreement about the phenomenon?
Clearly, the more straightforward the information, the fewer the number of interviews; the more complex the information that is sought,
the greater the number of interviews.

Semistructured Interviews

Semistructured interviews were described in detail in Chapter 8. The
researcher uses semistructured interviews when he or she knows

enough about a topic to create the questions stems, but not enough to anticipate all of the possible responses. All participants are asked the same questions in the same order, although the researcher may ask probing questions during their responses.

Focus Group Interviews

When focus groups are used as a supplementary component, they are usually fewer in number than when they are used as a core method (see Chapter 8). Again, the moderator's questions are prepared in advance—usually outlining the overall content and the information to be gained from the meetings. The group interview is controlled by the moderator, who asks the questions and probes and ensures that the interaction is balanced and not dominated by some members, so that others, who may be more reticent, can voice their opinions.

How many focus groups comprise a supplemental component? As with the interviews-as-a-supplemental-component, the number of focus groups depends on the nature of the information needed, the quality of the participants' knowledge, the willingness of the participants to inform the researchers about the phenomenon, and what role and contribution the knowledge obtained will contribute to the overall project. Again once, when the researcher has obtained the necessary information and the degree of certainty necessary, data collection ceases.

Participant Observation

Formal observations of the setting often provide necessary data to supplement the core method. Because of the unstructured nature of participant observation and the serendipitous nature of whatever is being observed, it is often difficult to "fit" observational data with a quantitative data set, and participant observations may be most usefully used in a sequential QUAN—>*qual* design, once the core data have been analyzed and specific questions remain to be answered.

Participant observation itself provides a great deal of variation in data collection. The role of the research as a member of the setting and action varies from complete noninvolvement to complete participation; the duration and timing of the observations and how the observations are recorded all affect the type of data recorded and the nature of the results. All of these factors must be planned in advance and negotiated with the research assistants. As with data collected for all supplemental components, how much data and how long the observations continue depend on the type of information needed, the complexity of the information being collected, and the contribution of the information to the overall project.

Processes of Conducting QUAN-*qual* Mixed Method Design

In this section, we present examples of various types of quantitatively-driven mixed method designs.

QUAN + *qual* Simultaneous Design

Quantitatively-driven simultaneous designs have a quantitative core component that is conducted with a qualitative supplemental component (see Figure 9.3). Although the quantitative sample is an adequate size for the supplementary component, it has been randomly selected so that, if this sample is used for the qualitative component, some thought must be given to the selection of participants from the quantitative sample. It is a mistake to select them randomly, for those selected may not have the experiences and information needed for the quantitative component; further, they may not have the "qualities of the good informant" (previously discussed), nor be willing to participate in the study. Therefore, the sample should be selected using the principles of qualitative inquiry. Data for the qualitative component are collected and analyzed separately from the quantitative core, but once the analysis is completed, they are combined with the quantitative narrative at the results point of interface.

QUAN + *qual* to Confirm

In a sample of 202 African American women with low level literacy skills (estimated at < 6th grade by the *Rapid Estimate of Adult Literacy in Medicine*) ($n=33$) and higher level literacy skills ($n=120$), 101 (50%) had inadequate utilization of prenatal care as estimated by the *Adequacy of Prenatal care Utilization Index*. Results show that literacy was not associated with prenatal care utilization, but rather communication with physicians was important. Women valued physicians who provided information "with clarity in simple pieces."

Example:
Bennet, I., Switzer, J., Aguirre, A., Evans, K., & Barg, F. (2006). "Breaking it down": Patient-clinician communication and prenatal care among African American women of low and higher literacy. *Annals of Family Medicine, 4*(4), 334–340.

Design	Theoretical drive: Deductive	Pacing: Sequential
	QUAN component: measure of "adequacy of prenatal care"	*qual* component: free listing (cultural domain analysis), interviews and focus groups
	Point of Interface: Results	

QUAN + *qual* to Enhance Description or Explain

Quantitative measures may not account for the phenomenon completely. The researcher may suspect that, for example the quantitative survey does not allow for a comprehensive assessment and that there

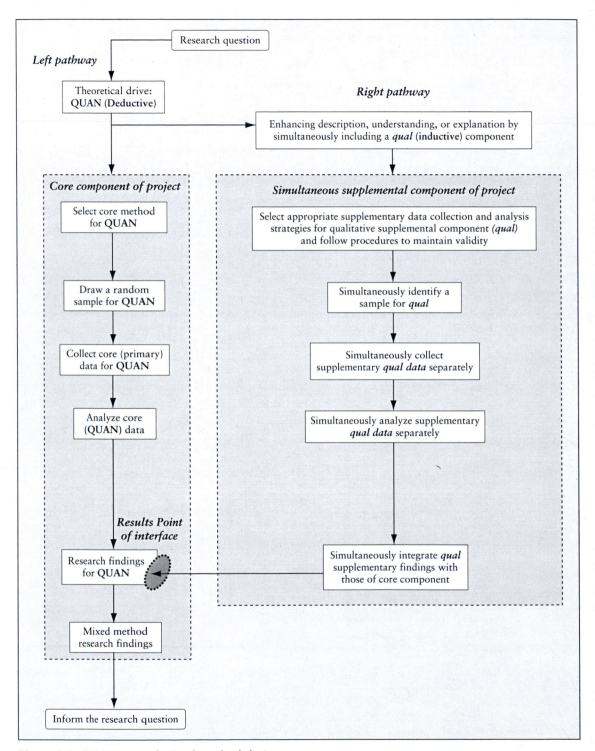

Figure 9.3 QUAN + *qual* mixed method design

are gaps or information that will be omitted. Further, the researchers may recognize that although they know what questions should be asked to fill these gaps, they cannot with any confidence preassign all possible answers to these questions, and for this reason open-ended questions should be used.

The researcher can insert such open-ended questions into the survey and content analyze these questions to provide the information needed—which is then interfaced into the analysis in the Results section.

But the researcher may also numerically code the open-ended questions that are included as a part of the survey questions so they may be transformed into quantitative variables and analyzed in the quantitative data set, enhancing descriptions or explanation (see Figure 9.4).

Data Transformation

What types of data lend themselves to transformation for QUAN + *qual*? How can transformation be done without violating the assumptions of the underlying method? Careful consideration of these issues is crucial for maintaining validity and the pacing of this process is shown in Figure 9.4.

The transformation process of qualitative data entails four steps (see, for example, Bernard, 2000):

- Step 1: Use techniques of content analyses to analyze textual responses (i.e., synthesize the qualitative data to its skeletal structure). Read the data purposively to see what is there. The researcher should become familiar with the data by highlighting or underlining phrases, making notes, and then identifying mutually exclusive response categories for each variable that emerges from the qualitative data. Actual words from respondents could be used to label these categories.

- Step 2: Develop a codebook by summarizing meanings of various codes and instructions used to code the responses obtained from participants for all the items in the questionnaire. Define and label each variable, including those that emerged from the textual data. Choose a unique name and label for each variable (i.e., in accordance with the rules of SPSS for assigning names and labels to variables). Label and list the response categories for each variable (value labels) and assign a numerical code (value) for each response category.

- Step 3: Establish interrater reliability.

- Step 4: Code textual responses obtained from participants by comparing each response with the possible response categories of a variable and recording the numerical code of the appropriate response category into which this response fits. Recheck interrater reliability periodically.

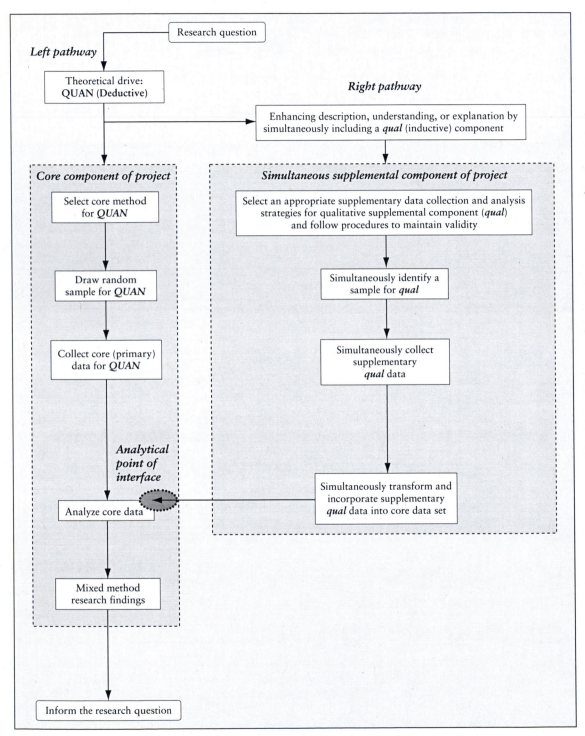

Figure 9.4 QUAN + *qual* mixed method design with data transformation

For QUAN + *qual designs*, these codes are imported as variables into the QUAN data set at the beginning of the data analysis, consistent with the quantitative theoretical drive of the project. Each qualitative item is then treated as a variable and, depending on the sample size and the level of data, analyzed using parametric or nonparametric statistics. Again, the results are used to enhance the description of quantitative findings and discussion of implications by indicating whether there are significant associations between relevant variables.

One Final Reminder

Often the nature of qualitative data has inherent characteristics that make the data unsuitable for numerical transformation. Data cannot be transformed and analyzed quantitatively if the researcher has used unstructured, nonstandardized interviews that have evolved as the study has progressed, as is often the case in ethnography, grounded theory, or phenomenology.

Example: An example of this simultaneous quantitatively-driven mixed method design is a quantitative Internet survey that was conducted to determine the incidence and severity of untoward effects of unstructured interviews for participants participating in qualitative research (Morse, Niehaus, & Varnhagen in preparation). The survey had approximately 10% of the items written as semistructured open-ended questions, used to address gaps in the quantitative survey used in the QUAN component. As the research literature referred to the use of unstructured interviews and researchers' awareness of potential harm from participant distress that may occur during these interviews, the theoretical drive or overall direction of the inquiry was deductive and quantitative.

Although the sample size of 517 respondents was not extraordinary large for the management of the numerical data, transposing these qualitative questions to enable their incorporation into the statistical analysis was a very large task. However, because there was limited response to each question, it was possible, and the inductive qualitative component greatly enhanced the validity of the overall project and enabled description or explanation of the phenomenon under investigation. For instance, qualitative questions were developed to address why some research topics could be labeled as "emotionally sensitive" topics.

Four response categories for this variable emerged from the data. These data revealed that during interviews, participants recalled feelings about "self issues," "controversial issues," "illness and/or caregiving issues," and "mental health issues." For coding all textual responses, it was also necessary to include the following response categories: "other issues," "more than one of the above," "Not applicable/Difficult to tell/Don't know." A numerical code was then assigned to each response category and this variable was included in the code book instructions for coding of the responses. The loss of detail that occurred with quantitative transposition is costly to the overall meaning, but it does contribute a different type of information provided.

Nevertheless, to compensate for this, the qualitative responses were also analyzed qualitatively using content analysis.

QUAN—>*qual* Sequential Design

Occasionally, following analysis, a researcher might obtain surprising and unexpected results from a quantitative survey or additional questions may arise, and the decision might then be made to add a qualitative component to address these issues.

Because the quantitative study has been completed, the quantitative sample is usually not available for the researchers, and a new qualitative sample must be drawn. Once more: The qualitative component is then conducted according to the principles of qualitative inquiry, and after analysis, the results are integrated into the core quantitative results. This design is shown on Figure 9.5.

In the following QUAN—>*qual* study exploring gender and social capital in Australia, the author suggests that the quantitative component provides the "big picture" (Hodgkin, 2008, p. 296), and the person's story provides "depth and texture."

Given that many empirical investigations regarding social capital have been documented in the literature across countries and across disciplines, the main study or *core component* of this project was guided by a deductive *theoretical drive* (QUAN) and a sequential qualitative component. The *research question* was: "Do men and women have different social capital profiles?" The QUAN component was designed to identify patterns of social, community, and civic participation for men and women and to illuminate issues of need. Once the *core component* (QUAN) was completed, a *supplemental component* (*qual*) was initiated to enhance description of women's underlying motivation for their participation in activities. In addition, the supplemental component (*qual*) "gave voice" to any issues of need by addressing the *question*: "Why do women participate more in social and community activities than in civic communities?" The *pacing* of the core and supplemental components was, therefore, sequential.

The *primary method* for collecting core data was a cross-sectional survey that was administered at one point in time. A sample of 4,000 households was randomly drawn and 403 men and 998 women, aged 18 and older, completed the survey. Descriptive and multivariate analyses were conducted on these core data.

For the *supplemental* (*qual*) *component*, data were collected by conducting in-depth one-on-one interviews with participants. The core sample was available for selecting participants for the *supplemental component* (*qual*)—of the 998 women who completed the questionnaire (*core sample*), 75 provided informed consent to be interviewed—but one limitation is that the researchers used cluster random sampling. "Already formed groups of individuals within the population" were used as sampling units to select a final sample of 12 women, aged 29 to 49, as participants for conducting the *supplementary* (*qual*) *component* who were interviewed twice. On the

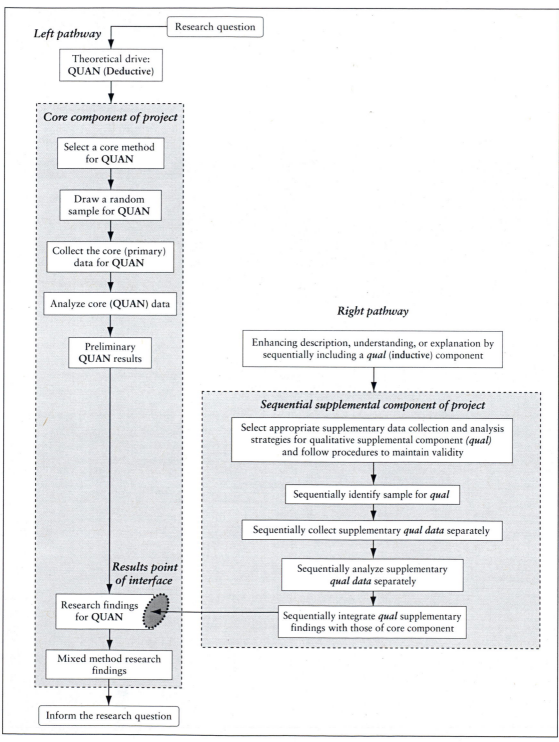

Figure 9.5 QUAN—>*qual* mixed method design

first occasion, an interview guide was used to collect data on these women's daily lives. They were then asked to document a week in their lives, and this was used as a starting point for the second interview. Transcripts of these supplemental data were analyzed using techniques of narrative analysis.

The *point of interface* of the core and supplemental components of this project was in the results narrative. Sampling, data collection, and analysis for the core (QUAN) and supplemental components (*qual*) were conducted separately and sequentially. As well, findings for each component were documented separately. The author then integrated the supplementary findings with those of the core component, adding literature, in the Discussion section, so that the qualitative findings enhanced understanding of the core results. Explaining the strength of mixed method design, the researcher indicated that the quantitative methods provided a statistical overview of participations, and the qualitative provided a "deeper story and helped enhanced the findings" (Hodgkin, 2008, p. 314).

Example: A QUAN—>qual design
Hodgkin, S. (2008). Telling it all: A story of women's social capital using a mixed methods approach. *Journal of Mixed Method Research*, 2(4), 296–316.

Design	Theoretical drive: Deductive Pacing: Sequential
	QUAN component: Survey *qual* component: interviews
	Point of Interface: Results

QUAN-*quan* Mixed Method Design

What is QUAN-*quan* mixed method design? If quantitative social science research usually contains more than one measurement instrument, then surely labeling such research makes no sense and "muddies the waters."

True.

But, in agreement with Yin (2006), we consider two components from the same paradigm to be included as a mixed method to address combinations of different types of measurement: physiological measure and a survey in the same project, for instance. The design may also be used if the QUAN—>*quan* components are separated by time, and, as in the example below, for evaluation.

As with the QUAL-*qual* design, the QUAN-*quan* flowcharts for simultaneous (QUAN + *quan*) and sequential designs are similar to the QUAN-*qual* (Figures 9.3 and 9.4), with *quan* substituted in the right pathway. As the samples for both the core and the supplemental components are large and randomized, if the samples are available, they may be shared for both components. We have drawn the samples for both designs with separate analysis, but, for the simultaneous design, there may be occasions in which the supplemental quantified data may be incorporated into the core analysis.

Physicians in a large practice of 17 primary care clinics wanted to test if the implementation of a chronic care model (CCM) resulted in improvement in the quality of care. They used a before-after design with a modified assessment of chronic illness care survey that rates 28 aspects of care for three conditions (diabetes, coronary heart disease, and depression). Next, they used administrative health claim data that could measure care to 90% of the clinic patients with insurance and used a regression model for each change in score associated with the quality measures.

Although the physicians appeared to have improved their practice as a result of implementing the CCM model, the improvement in patients with these conditions was slight. They authors concluded that they needed more sensitive, reliable, and valid measures, a larger sample, and more time to show changes.

Example:
Solberg, L. I., Crain, A. L., Sperl-Hillen, J. M., Hroscikoski, M. C., Engerbreston. K. I., & O'Connor, P. J. (2006). Care quality and implementation of the chronic care model: A quantitative study. *Annals of Family Medicine*, 4(4), 310–316.

Design	Theoretical drive: Deductive	Pacing: Sequential
	QUAN component: Survey	*quan* component:
	Point of Interface: Results	Administrative data

Writing up QUAN-*qual* Designs

On completion of the study, when writing the results, readers (and reviewers) need to be able to see the results from each component—which Teddlie and Tashakkori (2009) call *each strand*. This enables the findings from the quantitative core and the supplemental component to be evaluated and assessed. The quantitative components may include tables showing results and the qualitative sections, according to the methods used, should explain, for instance, the categories or themes identified. Then the author must write the result narrative—several paragraphs synthesizing the quantitative and the qualitative data—into a coherent statement.

Occasionally, authors present their mixed methods this way, but because in a conventional format there is no category for the synthesized results narrative, they place such results in the Discussion section. The Discussion section is not the place for results—this section should follow the qualitative and quantitative results (perhaps labeled as "Preliminary Findings"), and the combine results should be profiled as "Synthesized Results" or "Combined Results" or even "Mixed Methods Results." Then the Discussion section may follow, with the normal discussion of the contribution of your study to the literature, the strengths and weaknesses of the study, the limitations, implications and application, and perhaps where future research should be directed.

A Final Comment on QUAN-*qual* designs

Quantitatively-driven designs are more common and appear more rigorous than the qualitatively-driven designs discussed in Chapter 8. Perhaps this is because there are more quantitative researchers than qualitative ones. Perhaps it is also because it is easier to get funded for a quantitative study than a qualitative one. Both simultaneous and sequential designs are being used. It appears that QUAN mixed method designs will make important contributions in the future.

10

Complex Mixed and Multiple Method Designs

In this chapter, we discuss complex designs that are extensions of, or exceptions to, the mixed method designs already discussed in Chapters 8 and 9. These are designs that continue to add components beyond the designs described earlier (referred to by Teddlie and Tashakkori [2006] as "multi-strand"), or projects that continue to be linked as a series of mixed methods studies that become *multiple methods* research programs. Recall that multiple method designs are a series of completed studies cohesively linked to address the same programmatic research question, contributing in a stepwise fashion to solve a programmatic research goal.

QUAL Qualitatively-Driven Complex Designs

Mixed method design can become extremely complex, with supplemental components added to the theoretical core project in any combination, qualitative and quantitative, and used sequentially or simultaneously.

Complex Simultaneous Mixed Method Design: Ethnography

We have said that ethnography is a mixed method design because it consists of several strategies, used at various times during the conduct of the core method—which may consist primarily of unstructured interviews or observations. Because of this lack of structure and because it is not usually considered a mixed method, ethnography is not usually included in books describing mixed method designs. However, solving an ethnographic puzzle is an excellent way to understand both the complexity and the power of mixed method design. In this next section, we will walk through such an ethnographic study, which was to explore the cultural perception of pain and the various differing behaviors of different cultures toward the same pain stimulus (Morse, 1989).

Persons from different cultural groups have different responses to similar pain stimuli. In this project, I examined the cultural response to the pain of childbirth manifested by Fijians and Fiji-Indians. The ethnography was conducted in the obstetrical unit of a hospital in Fiji, and included pre- and postpartum interviews with mothers and nurses, observations and physical recording during birth, interviews in the community with traditional birth attendants, and a finally, a questionnaire to measure the perceived pain of childbirth, administered to a larger sample of postpartum mothers and members in the community.

Initially, ethnography is exploratory. Interviews were conducted with traditional birth attendants, and these provided insights into the values and beliefs regarding traditional birth in both the Fiji-Indian and the Fijian cultures. Next, observations in the delivery room revealed very different behaviors for the Fijian and the Fiji-Indian mothers—differences in movements, vocalizations, and responses to the pain of delivery. Third, interviews with first-time mothers in early labor revealed differences in expectations about the imminent birth, and interviews with and observations of nurses providing care revealed that assessing pain was not a conscious evaluation of the manifest pain behaviors. Finally, the construction of a quantitative psychometric scale to assess the amount of pain perceived to be associated with childbirth in general (when compared with other painful events) revealed that not only were pain expectations culturally learned, transmitted, and associated with pain behaviors (Zborowski, 1969), but also *how painful* an event was rated was consistent within a particular cultural group, varied between cultures, and associated with the traditional cultural practices to manage the pain.

Table 10.1 lists the data collection process for this study. Notice that some of the data collection strategies began early in the study and were completed midway during the study, whereas others began later in the process. Some of the strategies were terminated because they were uninterpretable and did not yield useful data; others were developed as the study progressed and the need to obtain certain types of information arose; others were developed to explore glimpses of insights learned earlier parts of the study; and others were developed to confirm hunches. Thus, doing ethnography is like solving a puzzle—abductive detective work at its best.

Example:
Morse, J. M. (1989). Cultural responses to parturition: Childbirth in Fiji. *Medical Anthropology, 12*(1), 35–44.

Design	Theoretical drive: Inductive QUAL components: Interviews, Observations Point of Interface: Results	Pacing: Sequential *quan* component: Instrument

QUAL + *qual* + *quan*—>*qual* + *qual*—>*quan*

Table 10.1 Ethnographic Reflexive-Emergent QUAL Design

Proposal: QUAL + *qual* + *quan*

Components	Proposal	Planned Data — Data	Early in data collection — Data	Beginning understanding — Data	Stage of Comprehension — Data	Stage of Conjecture/ Confirmation — Data	Cultural pain expectations — Data	Final analysis Interpretation & conceptualization — Results
Contextual data	Literature	Preliminary cultural framework					*Qual* Additional data from newspaper	Framework developed
	Descriptions of traditional birth	QUAL Interviews with TBAs	Good	Excellent	Excellent- provided insights	No longer necessary		Important
Pain expectation	Descriptions of birth expectation	Interviews in early labor	Poor	Stopped. Used as "*negative*" confirmation		Staff informed. Nurses confirmed	*qual* Interviews with nurses	Significant
Documentation of pain behaviors in labor	Observation of behavior & indices of pain	Behavioral codes	OK	OK	Ceased		*quan* Measurement confirm. of cultural pain expectation	Observations confirm. Cultural measure of pain expectation important
		Vocalizations (taped)	OK but sometimes environmental noise too loud	OK but sometimes drowned out	*qual*			

Table 10.1 *Cont'd*

Proposal: QUAL + *qual* + *quan*

Components	Proposal	Planned Data	Early in data collection	Beginning understanding	Stage of Comprehension	Stage of Conjecture/Confirmation	Cultural pain expectations	Final analysis Interpretation & conceptualization
			Data	Data	Data	Data	Data	Results
	Physiological measures of pain and duration of second stage	Pulse	OK	OK	Ceased	*Physiological measures uninterpretable*		
		B/p	OK	OK	Ceased			
		PTT	Malfunction	Ceased				
		Timing of second stage contraction						
		Analgesics	OK	OK	*quan* Hypothesis Developed & confirmed from patient record data			Chart data added confirmatory information
		Cervical dilation	OK	OK				
Confirmation of pain experience	Postdelivery	Interviews	Poor	Stopped				Not used
Studies contributing to analysis	QUAL				+*qual* +*quan*		—>*qual* + *qual* —>*quan*	
Final design	QUAL + *qual* + *quan*—>*qual* +*qual*—>*quan*							

Complex Mixed Method Designs Versus Research Programs Consisting of Mixed Methods Projects

Can mixed methods research projects become extensive enough to form a research program? Of course they can. Mixed method studies may consist of a large number of components as a single extensive study, or several mixed method studies, or a collection of single method and mixed method studies.

What links these studies together? It is the AIM of the overall research program that makes it a cohesive whole. Addressing the larger programmatic AIM gives the research program its *theoretical thrust*, an overall inductive or deductive perspective, similar, but larger than the theoretical drive. As with the theoretical drive, this overall perspective overrides any deductive projects within the program, so that if the program has an inductive theoretical trust and includes a quantitative project, the overall direction of the thrust is not altered.

> The *theoretical thrust* is the overall inductive/deductive direction of the programmatic aim of a multiple method research program.

An important point: Studies that form these programs may be published in different research journals and be published out of synchrony. Ideally, they should refer to the other studies in the set, but they may not necessarily do so.

This complex mixed method, qualitatively-driven design was used in an article on bullying (Kulig, Hall, & Kalischuk, 2008). The primary study (QUAL) was guided by an inductive *theoretical drive* to obtain a much needed understanding of how youth in rural settings in Western Canada perceive "bullying," which could be regarded as a form of violence. Semistructured interviews were conducted to collect data for the qualitative *core component* (QUAL) of the study. The interview guide that was used to collect these data included questions for obtaining demographic information from participants and open-ended questions on definitions of violence, such as: "Is violence psychological in nature?" A total of 52 male and female participants from two health regions in Alberta were interviewed. The data were then analyzed. The *point of interface* between this qualitative phase and the next phase of the research, was in the research narrative.

Based on the qualitative findings obtained, a survey instrument was developed for conducting the quantitative phase of the research that appears to be quite complete and much more than just complementary to the core component. In fact, this "phase" of the research could rather be regarded as a "related project" for which a QUAN + *qual* mixed method design was used. This survey included 70 questions on violence-related topics (QUAN), as well as open-ended questions related to "bullying" (*qual*). A separate sample of 180 participants, randomly drawn from study population at two rural schools in different geographic areas, completed the survey. Statistical analyses were performed on the quantitative data.

It is not quite clear how the responses to the open-ended questions were analyzed. Using a QUAN + *qual* design requires an *analytical point of interface* for maintaining validity. Given that the sample (both selection and size) for the supplemental qualitative component (*qual*) was the same as for the primary quantitative component (QUAN), textual responses to semistructured, open-ended questions may be transposed to quantitative data and incorporated into the core quantitative data set *prior* to data analysis, consistent with the overall deductive theoretical drive of what appears to be a "related quantitative project."

Example: QUAL—>*quan + qual*
Kulig, J. C., Hall, B.I. & Kalischuk, R.G. (2008). Bullying perspectives among rural youth: a mixed-methods approach. *Rural and Remote Health, 8,* 923. (Online).

| Design | Theoretical drive: Inductive QUAL component: semi-structured interviews Point of Interface: Results | Design Pacing: Sequential + simultaneous *quan* component: questionnaire |

Quantitatively-Driven Complex Mixed Method Designs

An example of this quantitatively-driven design was reported in an article on HIV testing and care in Aboriginal communities (Mill et al., 2008). This research project comprised of a quantitative *core component* (QUAN) and *two* qualitative *sequential components* (*qual*), aimed at addressing three key questions: "Why do Aboriginal youth have an HIV test? What are the testing behaviours of Aboriginal youth and what types of services do they use? Among Aboriginal youth, what is the relationship between HIV testing and the decision to initiate treatment?" The researchers followed a community-based approach to address these issues.

The *core component* of this project, which entailed a self-administered survey, was guided by a deductive *theoretical drive* (QUAN). Supplementary qualitative data (*qual*) were *simultaneously* collected by including open-ended items in the survey. A total of 413 Aboriginal youth from Vancouver, Edmonton, Winnipeg, Ottawa, Toronto, Montreal, Halifax, Labrador, and Inuvik participated in this survey.

A *sequential component* (*qual*) consisting of semistructured interviews was then initiated to enhance description, understanding or explanation of HIV testing and care decisions of Canadian Aboriginal youth. Data were collected by conducting semistructured interviews with 28 participants and analyzed using a coding framework that was developed inductively. The *pacing* of this supplemental component is, therefore, sequential.

The *point of interface* of the core and supplemental components of this project seem to be in the research narrative. Sampling, data collection, and analysis for the core (QUAN) and *second* supplemental component (*qual*) were done separately and sequentially. The authors integrate the supplementary findings with those of the core component by pointing out how findings obtained by interviewing Aboriginal youth enhanced understanding of the survey (core) findings.

Example: QUAN + *qual* + *qual*

Mill, J. E., Jackson, R. C., Worthington, C. A., Archibald, C. P., Wong, T., Myers, T., Prentice, T., & Sommerfeldt, S. (2008). HIV testing and care in Canadian Aboriginal youth: A community based mixed methods study. BMC *Infectious Diseases*, 8, 132 doi:10.1186/1471-2334-8-132.

Design	Theoretical drive: Deductive	Pacing: Sequential
	QUAL component: Survey (including open-ended questions)	*quan* component: Semistructured interviews
		Point of Interface: Results

Multiple Method Research Programs

Multiple method research programs are defined as a series of inter-related studies conducted to address one programmatic aim. The programmatic *aim* gives the research program its *theoretical thrust,* which drives the program. The first project indicating the theoretical thrust, is listed in CAPS (e.g., QUAL); because subsequent studies are complete and under the rubric of the same theoretical thrust, we list them also in caps but in small font (e.g., QUAN for a quantitative project). If the subsequent project is a mixed method project, we include the project in square brackets (see Box 10.1). For instance, a multiple method project may consist of qualitative study, followed by a quantitative sequential *qual* mixed method project, and then a quantitative project. This would appear as:

QUAL—>[QUAN—>*qual*] —>QUAN

Another example: Suppose that the *aim* of your hypothetical project was inductive, the theoretical thrust inductive and the first project QUAL; the second project conducted simultaneously, was quantitative QUAN with a qualitative supplemental component *qual* followed by a sequential QUAN study with a supplemental *quan* component. This would be diagrammed as: QUAL + [QUAN + *qual*]—>[QUAN + *quan*].

Multiple method studies usually contribute to the overall aim in an incremental fashion, but because each study is complete in itself and are often published in different journals, until a review article synthesizes the results, the contributions may be difficult to identify.

Rather than building stepwise, some multiple method programs build laterally, side by side, increasing the scope of the problem that is being addressed. Because these studies are complete, they are also frequently published in different journals, and sometimes the first article does not even refer to other publications in the same set. Consequently, with such research programs it is often difficult to identify all the

---

Box 10.1 Terminology for Multiple Method Design

Multiple method design	A *scientifically rigorous* research program *comprised of a series of related qualitative and/or quantitative* research projects over time, *driven by the* theoretical thrust *of the program. The theoretical drive of an individual project may on occasion counter but not change the overall inductive or deductive direction of the entire program.*
Method	A cohesive combination of methodological strategies or set of research tools that is inductively or deductively used in conducting qualitative or quantitative inquiry.
Theoretical thrust	The overall inductive or deductive direction of a research program. The nature of the overall programmatic research question determines the theoretical thrust of the research program. The theoretical drive of an individual project may on occasion counter but not change the theoretical thrust of the research program.
Multimethod design	A plan for a scientifically rigorous research program comprised of a series of related qualitative and/or quantitative research projects over time, driven by the theoretical thrust of the program. The theoretical drive of an individual project may on occasion counter but not change the overall inductive or deductive direction of the entire program.

"pieces" addressed by the author (Morse & Niehaus, 2007). Note, however, that these are *not* studies from one large project that the investigator has "split" at the moment of publication. These projects are *not* usually the product of "salami slicing," or the splitting of a single study to increase the number of articles so that sometimes, when publishing two or more articles from the same study, some of the publications may be thin and weak.

As stated, in multiple method research programs each study addresses a different research question within the same broad programmatic aim. These studies may (but not always) use a different method within the same research program, and each study is methodologically and substantively complete in itself (see Figure 10.1).

However, a multiple method set of research studies may include qualitative and/or quantitative studies and even mixed method studies. These articles tend to appear in different journals, and the various publication lags from different journals often results in these articles being published "out of synch," so that sometimes articles conducted earlier in the research program are published later than subsequent

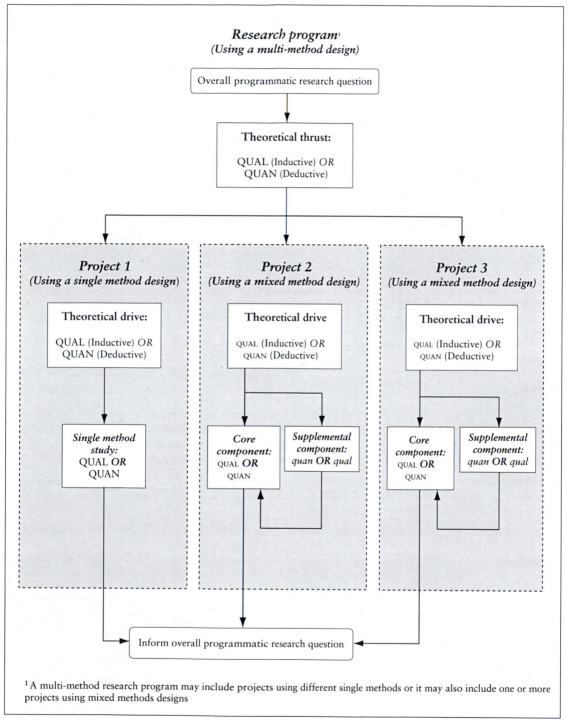

Figure 10.1 An example of a multiple method research program

work. Further, some may be listed in different databases, and readers may be unaware of certain key articles—especially if the author has not cited them. To overcome this problem, some research groups list an acronym for their research program in the author list, so readers could search for their articles in the citation listings in the databases. Sometimes researchers publish a comprehensive summary article—or even a book—pulling the results of the research program together in a cohesive whole, to clarify the contributions of the works, to generate theory, or to clarify the implications.

This sequential qualitatively-driven multiple method design was used for exploring the choices and decisions women in urban Thailand make regarding child care (Richter, 1997/2008). Existing literature on child care revealed that little has been documented about these decision-making processes women go through to make child care choices for dealing with employment-related issues. The *theoretical drive* that guided the qualitative *core project* (QUAL) was, therefore, inductive. This *qualitative core* (QUAL) was aimed at developing a model of child care decision making. As well, a second *supplemental quantitative study* (QUAN) was conducted after the model of child care decision-making was developed. The role of this *supplemental study* (QUAN) was to add a second layer of description to the *core* qualitative component (QUAL) by testing the model. Hence, the core and supplemental components were sequentially *paced* or synchronized (see Table 10.2).

The *primary sample* comprised of women who were selected from three types of employment, or who were not employed. Core data were collected by conducting in-depth interviews and focus groups. These data were then analyzed and, based on the results, a model of child care decision making was developed.

These findings were then followed by a quantitative *supplemental project* (QUAN): a quantitative instrument can be administered to the participants in the core qualitative sample or to another equivalent purposefully selected qualitative sample, provided the same criteria for its selection are used. A representative sample of 1,515 married women was drawn to participate in a household survey. Multivariate analyses were conducted on the quantitative data obtained.

The *point of interface* of the core and supplemental project was in the research narrative. The researcher described how the findings from the household survey (QUAN) enhanced description and understanding of the model of child care decision making.

Example: A Multiple Method Design. Adolescents responses to menarche

Table 10.2 Schematic outline of QUAL—>QUAN multiple method project

Study 1		Study 2		Results
Interviews & focus groups	—>	Household survey	=	Integrate findings in results narrative

The overall aim of this qualitatively-driven multiple method research program was to determine adolescent responses to menarche. This is an exploratory aim, and it is this that gives the research program an inductive theoretical drive. The five studies that build the research program are listed in Table 10.3. Based on a qualitative study, the qualitative theoretical drive moved the study from a basic exploratory study, through the development of a Likert scale, to hypothesis testing. The study may therefore be described as a QUAL—>QUAL—>QUAN—> QUAN—>QUAN.

Example: A QUAL—>QUAN Multiple Method Design
Richter, K. (1997/2008). Child-care choice in urban Thailand: Qualitative and quantitative evidence of the decisions making process. *Journal of Family Issues*, 18(2) 174–204. Reprinted in *The mixed methods reader*, V. L. Plano Clark & J. W. Creswell, eds. (pp. 550-582). Thousand Oaks, CA: Sage.

QUAL—>QUAN Multiple Method Research Program

Example: Qualitatively-driven, multiple method research program to explore fatigue

Study 1 (QUAL)

In a concept analysis of fatigue, based on research literature drawn from five populations who experienced fatigue for different reasons (cancer, chronic fatigue syndrome, depression, shift workers, recreational runners), Olson and Morse (2005) reconceptualized fatigue as three distinct concepts—tiredness, fatigue, and exhaustion. These were related to each other in a manner consistent with stress theory, but could be distinguished from each other based on qualitative differences in six important dimensions—stamina (muscle endurance), cognitive function, sleep quality, control over body processes, emotional reactivity, and social network. Using this information, Olson and Morse (2005) formulated the fatigue adaptation model.

Study 2 (QUAL)

Following further analysis of fatigue based on qualitative data collected in cancer and palliative care populations (Olson, Krawchuk, & Quddusi, 2007), Olson et al. (2008) identified a new concept—*adaptive capacity*—defined as the internal resources that one can mobilize to adapt to stressors. They then further refined the fatigue adaptation model (*quan*) to create the Edmonton fatigue framework (EFF). Within the EFF, adaptive capacity is a function of the combined impact of muscle endurance, cognitive function, sleep quality, emotional reactivity, social network, and dietary intake (Olson et al., 2008).

Table 10.3 Multiple method research program with an inductive thrust (QUAL)

Study	Title	Role
#1 Inductive QUAL	Morse, J. M., & Doan, H. M. (1987). Growing up at school: Adolescents' response to menarche. *Journal of School Health, 57*(9), 385–389.	Qualitative content analysis Identified categories of responses toward menarche. Provided phrases and language that formed the basis of the Likert scale items.
#2 Inductive QUAL	Morse, J. M., Kieren, D., & Bottorff, J. L. (1993). The Adolescent Menstrual Attitude Questionnaire, I: Scale Construction. *Health Care for Women International, 14*, 39–62.	Development of the scale— used identified categories as hypothesized factors and developed items
#3 Deductive QUAN	Morse, J. M., & Kieren, D. (1993). The Adolescent Menstrual Attitude Questionnaire, Part II: Normative Scores. *Health Care for Women International, 14*, 63–76.	Determined validity of questionnaire Extended our understanding about menarche by examining the distribution of symptoms and attitudes of adolescent girls in the population to determine normative scores
#4 QUAN	Kieren, D., & Morse, J. M. (1992). Preparation factors and menstrual attitudes of pre- and postmenarcheal girls. *Journal of Sex Education and Therapy, 18*, 155–174.	Scale "in use"
#5 QUAN	Kieren, D. K., & Morse, J. M. (1995). Developmental factors and pre- and post-menarcheal menstrual attitudes. *Canadian Home Economics Journal, 45*(2), 61–67.	Scale "in use"

Study 3 (QUAN)

A tool to assess fatigue by measuring adaptive capacity is currently in development, but initial testing shows that the structure of the tool is consistent with the hypotheses of the EFF. This sequential research program may be expressed as: QUAL—>QUAL—>QUAN.

Multiple Methods for Developing Theory

If, for example, we are trying to understand a very broad and encompassing concept, such as suffering, then we could conduct a number of studies using different populations who are suffering, using interview data (Morse & Johnson, 1991), and from this work constructed a general model of the process inherent in suffering (enduring and emotional suffering) and how people move through this trajectory (Morse, 2001, 2005; Morse & Carter, 1996).

Next, we could conduct observational studies of patients at various parts of the model, such as patients in pain (Morse & Mitcham, 1997) or micro-analytic studies of infant pain (Côté, Morse, & James, 1991), or trauma resuscitation (Morse & Proctor, 1998); we could conduct studies to see what would happen if, for instance, enduring failed (Dewar & Morse, 1995). We could conduct studies of various patient population experiences at various points in the model, such as enduring to die (Olson, Morse, Smith, et al., 2000–2001), or as they move through the model, for instance, transition between enduring and emotional suffering (Morse et al., 2003). We could use the literature to conduct abstract concept analyses of the varying subconcepts within suffering, such as hope (Morse & Doberneck, 1995).

Because these studies of smaller components are all a part of an overall scheme of the phenomenon of suffering, they should fit together logically, as pieces of a puzzle fit into a larger picture. In fact, we might also deliberately explore parts of the model for which we know must exist but for which we do not have information. For instance, we had only one "healthy" exit point from emotional suffering, but we wanted to know if people could also exit for enduring. So we tried to think of a "naturalistic experiment" in which people were enduring, then whatever they were enduring was removed so they did not have to emotionally suffer. The best example we could think of was women undergoing diagnosis for breast cancer; we then explored the responses of those who were positive with those who were negative. Yes, the model may be exited as *relief*.

Fitting all of these projects together—projects conducted on different populations from neonates to the palliative patient, from patients and relatives, from mild discomfort to various states of agony, from slow onset to acute—all contributed to *Toward a Praxis Theory of Suffering* (Morse, 2001).

Notes on the Principles of Mixed Method Design

Table 10.4 Notes on Principles of Mixed Method Design

Principle #1:	Work with as few data sets as possible.
	Parsimony is perfection
	—assess base method and focus for completeness
	-boundary identified?
	-in-depth?
	-generalizable?
Principle #2:	The more you know about research methods, the easier mixed methods will be!
	Do an armchair walkthrough, *so you know where you are going and why*
	Always be aware of the direction you are working—inductively or deductively
Principle #3:	Recognize and respect the project's theoretical drive.
	The theoretical drive refers to the conceptual contribution of the core method—not which component comes first, not which component was the most work, not which component too the longest
	We call it a *drive* because it steers the project
	Remember you maybe actually working in the opposite direction—in a *qual* supplementary core in a QUAN project—or vice versa
Principle #4:	Recognize the role of the supplemental component.
	This component *supports* the core component—it does not compete
	The project is enriched because of the core component
Principle #5:	Adhere to the methodological assumptions of each method.
	Qualitative is qualitative: Quantitative is quantitative—do each well
Principle #6:	Carefully consider the pacing of the components.
	Make your research as efficient as possible, without compromising quality
	Diagram your study . . .
Principle #7:	Sampling must be compatible with the assumptions belonging to the method or strategy it serves.
	Qualitative is qualitative: Quantitative is quantitative. A slip can be very expensive!
Principle #8:	Mixed method design is systematic.
	It is not a salad!!! Components are not blended, embedded, nor wed

Table 10.4 *Cont'd*

Principle #9:	The two data sets separate until the point of interface. unless you are transposing. . .
Principle #10:	Adhere to the methodological assumptions of the core method. When working on core. . .
Principle #11:	The direction of theoretical drive is evident in the core component. But between the supplemental sample selection and the point of interface, the researcher must adhere to the paradigmatic assumptions of the supplemental method. Thinking differently for each component will become a way of life
Principle #12:	If you can measure, measure. Just keep any limitations in mind.
Principle #13:	Whatever is being coded and/or counted must make sense.
Principle #n:	The possibilities are endless. . .

Appendix I
Glossary for Mixed Method Designs

Box 1: Terminology for Mixed Method Design

Component	*A phase of the research, driven by the overall direction of the inquiry, during which one or more methodological strategies are used as research tools to address the research question.*
Core component of the project	*The primary (main) study in which the primary or core method is used to address the research question. This phase of the research is complete or scientifically rigorous and can therefore stand alone.*
Method	*A cohesive combination of methodological strategies or set of research tools that is inductively or deductively used in conducting qualitative or quantitative inquiry.*
Mixed method design	*A scientifically rigorous* research project, *driven by the inductive or deductive* theoretical drive, *and comprised of a qualitative or quantitative* core component *with qualitative or quantitative* supplementary component(s). *These supplementary components of the research fit together to enhance description, understanding, or explanation and can either be conducted simultaneously or sequentially with the core component. Mixed method design can also take place as internal transformation of a single data set.*
Pacing	*The mode in which the core and complementary component are synchronized.*
Point of interface	*The position in which the method and the supplemental component join—either in the data analysis or in the narrative of the results.*

Box 1 *Cont'd*

QUAL; QUAN	Upper case represents the project representing the theoretical thrust of the research program. QUAL indicates a qualitative theoretical thrust; QUAN indicates a quantitative theoretical thrust.
qual; quan	Lower case represents the project representing the supplemental component mixed method project. *qual* indicates a qualitative supplemental component; *quan* indicates a quantitative supplemental component.
Strategy	*A methodological research tool, drawn from a qualitative or quantitative method, for addressing the research question by either collecting and/or analyzing data.*
Supplementary component of the project	*In this phase of the research, one or more supplementary methodological strategies are used to obtain an enhanced description, understanding or explanation of the phenomenon under investigation. This component of the project can either be conducted at the same time as the core component (simultaneous) or it could follow the core component (sequential). The supplementary component is incomplete in itself or lacks some aspect of scientific rigor,* cannot stand alone, *and is regarded as complementary to the core component.*
Theoretical drive	*The overall inductive or deductive direction of a* research project *(Morse, 2003) that guides the use of the appropriate qualitative and/or quantitative methodological core. The nature of the* research question *determines the theoretical drive of a* project.

Morse, J. M., Wolfe, R., & Niehaus, L. (2006). Principles and procedures for maintaining validity for mixed method design. In Leslie Curry, Renée Shield & Terrie Wetle (Eds.), *Qualitative Methods in Research and Public Health: Aging and Other Special Populations* (pp. 65–78). Washington, DC: GSA and APHA. Printed with permission of the publisher.

Box 2: Terminology for Multiple Method Design

Multiple method design	*A scientifically rigorous* **research program** *comprised of a series of related qualitative and/or quantitative* **research projects over time***, driven by the* **theoretical thrust** *of the program. The theoretical drive of an individual project may on occasion counter but not change the overall inductive or deductive direction of the entire program.*
Method	A cohesive combination of methodological strategies or set of research tools that is inductively or deductively used in conducting qualitative or quantitative inquiry.
QUAL; QUAN	Small caps indicate the theoretical drive of a mixed method project embedded in a multiple method research program.

Box 2 *Cont'd*

Theoretical thrust	*The overall inductive or deductive direction of a* **research program**. *The nature of the* **overall programmatic research** *question determines the theoretical thrust of the* **research program**. *The theoretical drive of an individual project may on occasion counter but not change the theoretical thrust of the research program.*
[ ]	Square brackets delimit each mixed method project within a multiple method research program. For example, [QUAL + *quan*] indicates a qualitatively-driven mixed method study with a quantitative supplemental component, which is a part of a multiple method program.

Appendix II
Dissecting Mixed Method Publications

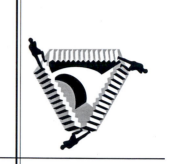

In Chapter 1, we discussed the problem of mixed method design commonly used in published research, with the components not identified or easily identifiable. As a result, these articles are often difficult to follow; sometimes, it is even difficult to grasp the process and procedures used in the project. To overcome this, we have developed this "dissection chart" so that the article may be systematically examined and the design clarified (see Chart 1.1). Those attending our workshops have reported that this is so useful that they use this scheme when they are planning their own projects.

The analysis of published article begins, of course, by reading the entire article. This gives you a "feel" for the article and it can save you time if you highlight as you read. Highlight the aim or goals of the research study, research question, the sample used for each component, and the methods used. Highlight the pacing of data collection and the points of interface.

Now to begin your analysis, examine the aim/goals of the study and the research question. Was the investigator working inductively or deductively? From this, you should be able to complete the first question: the *theoretical drive* used in the study.

The *core component* should be the primary part of the Aim(s) and the research question. Examine the fit between the research question and the core component—they should flow logically one from the other. If the theoretical drive is inductive, then the method used should be a qualitative method, or a statistical technique such as *EDA* (exploratory data analysis techniques [for example, see Tukey, 1977]). If the theoretical drive is deductive, then quantitative designs used the enable hypothesis or theory testing, or minimally descriptive statistics that enable the researchers to state how much or how many. In addition, the core component should be publishable by itself: It should meet research evaluation criteria for rigor by itself, without the supplementary component.

These criteria include validity and reliability which are most commonly used for evaluating quantitatively-driven research (Eun-Ok Im, et al., 2004), and the procedures for conducting the research, including the adequacy and appropriateness of the data collection and analysis (Morse, Swanson & Kuzel, 2001).

The *supplemental component* is not "complete" by itself and cannot be published without the core component. By this we mean that if it is a qualitative study, then the researchers has kept sampling until he or she has the answers to whatever they want to know, is *certain*, but may be been asking about a relatively small topic, rather than scoping a phenomenon, or may have stopped sampling before saturation was reached. The qualitative supplemental topic may not have been a formal qualitative method, such as a grounded theory, and is more likely to have been several focus groups or some semistructured survey questions.

The quantitative supplementary component for qualitatively-driven component may have been measurements of some relevant variables, but the sample size of the qualitative core component was too small to be able to even analyze these data using means, and an external norm must be used to interpret these scores. Alternatively, nonparametric statistics (Seigel & Castellan, 1988) may be used to analyze these data as a group, but the sample size and the nonrandom sample will make the findings tentative and best interpreted in the context of the study.

Next, note how the two components are combined. Is the *point of interface* in the data the analysis, so that the two data sets were combined and analyzed together, or is each component analyzed separately and the results of each combined in the results narrative? How does the supplemental component support the core component?

By now you should be able to name the type of mixed method design. Your descriptions should be something like this:

> *This is a quantitatively-driven, mixed method design with a simultaneous qualitative component: QUAN + qual.*

Or

> *This is a qualitatively-driven, mixed method design with a simultaneous quantitative component: QUAL + quan.*

Now, examine the *adequacy* of the study. Ask:

- *What was the nature of the phenomenon under study?*
- *Did the mixed method design enhance the comprehensiveness (understanding) of the phenomenon?*
- *Did it more clearly incorporate the scope?*
- *Did it enrich the description?*
- *Enable a more comprehensive understanding of relationships between variables?*

Now *evaluate the appropriate use of each method*. Were the assumptions belonging to each method adhered to, or were there some violations. For instance, were the principles of sampling for each method used correctly, or was, for instance the purposeful sample used for the quantitative component? If so, did this seriously impede the design or the results? Could the investigator have avoided making this error, or was it unavoidable?

Samples: If different participants were used for each component, were the two samples draw appropriately and were they from equivalent populations. Were the types of samples appropriate for each method? If the same samples were used, was the sample size adequate for each method? Did the nonrandomness of the QUAL sample interfere with the quantitative method? Or did the randomness of the QUAN sample interfere with the qualitative results. Generally, when a nonpurposive sample is used for qualitative inquiry, a larger sample is needed than if a purposive and theoretical sample is used. On the other hand, if a purposive sample is used to quantitative purposes, the investigator must examine the data carefully to see if any bias has occurred and if so, if this is harmful to the study conclusions.

Chart 1.1 Worksheet for analyzing MM research

Published Articles Reporting Mixed Method Design Research

Assignment: Please discuss and critique each article by addressing the questions/issues below.

Questions/Issues	Article 1	Article 2	Article 3	Article 4
1. Identify:				
• Theoretical drive				
• Core component				
• Supplemental component				
• Point(s) of interface				
Identify the type of MM design from flow chart–Figure 8.1 (for qualitatively-driven) or Figure 9.1 (for quantitatively-driven) designs)				

Questions/Issues	Article 1	Article 2	Article 3	Article 4
What is the nature of the phenomenon under investigation?				
Were the QUAL/QUAN methods/strategies appropriately used? Give reasons.				
What is the nature of the primary sample? Appropriate? Adequate?				
Did the supplementary component of the project require a different sample? If so, how was the appropriateness and adequacy of the new sample assured?				

Discuss the *points of interface*. Was the integration (fit) of the two components appropriate?

Consider the generalizability of the study. Has the author over/under generalized? Give reasons.

Evaluate the rigor of the study:

a) Can the core component stand alone?

b) Is the supplementary component adequate for the study purposes?

Questions/Issues	Article 1	Article 2	Article 3	Article 4
c) What violations to reliability and validity (if any) occurred?				
Outline the design of each MM article by drawing a flowchart.				

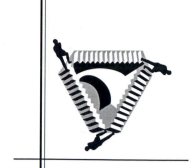

Appendix III
Search Filters for Retrieving Mixed Method Studies from Bibliographic Databases

Linda G. Slater

Search filters (also known as search hedges and canned searches) are searches designed to refine a subject search by retrieving a subset of the results that meet specific criteria (e.g., geographic areas, age groups, methodology). Relevant controlled vocabulary (also known as subject headings, descriptors, or thesaurus terms) as well as text-words/keywords (i.e., the author-derived terms that appear in the title and abstract of a bibliographic record) are incorporated into filters to ensure comprehensive retrieval. Searchers make use of a search filter by combining the results of the filter with the results of their initial subject search.

The methodology filters described in this section have been created to retrieve references to mixed method studies. They have been developed in consultation with experts in the area of mixed method research and by scanning database records of mixed method articles, noting the controlled vocabulary and text word terms used to describe the studies. The filters are intended to be comprehensive—that is, to retrieve as many mixed method studies as possible. That being the case, a number of references to nonmixed method studies will be retrieved along with references to studies that clearly are of the mixed method variety.

Issues that had to be considered when designing the filters include the following:

- Within this publication, the terms "mixed method" and "multiple method" research have been used as synonyms to describe a methodology that "draws inferences using both qualitative and quantitative approaches or methods in a single study or program of inquiry" (*Journal of Mixed Methods Research*, 2008). However, there appears to be no agreement among the broader community of researchers about the definition of the various terminology used to describe mixed method studies. Some researchers consider the terms "mixed method" and "multiple method" to be synonymous; others consider "mixed method" to refer to studies that combine qualitative and quantitative methods, whereas the term "multiple method" refers to studies that combine different methods within one of the two categories of qualitative and quantitative research (Johnson, Onwuegbuzie, & Turner, 2007). Because there is no consensus on the definition of these two terms, both terms (and their variants) are used in these filters to ensure comprehensiveness.
- Authors have not always used explicit terms like "mixed method," "multiple method," "multimethod," "mixed research," and so on when describing their methodology, even

though it is clear they have undertaken mixed method research. For that reason, terms had to be incorporated into the filters that represent the varied ways in which a mixed method study can be described in an article abstract. In some cases, these variant terms have different meanings depending on the context. For example, the terms "qualitative" and "quantitative" are used frequently in the literature of imaging technology but not in the same sense as mixed method researchers would use them; hence, depending on the subject searched, a number of off-topic imaging references may be retrieved along with more relevant items.

- Because authors do not always make it clear in their abstracts whether a "between/cross method" or "within method" of triangulation has been used in their study, the filter makes no attempt to differentiate between these types of triangulation. This will result in some studies being retrieved that use within- method triangulation and so would not be considered mixed method.

- The *ProQuest* interface is limited in the number of terms that can be searched simultaneously. Because the interface could not accommodate all the terms that should have been included to ensure comprehensiveness, the possibility of relevant items being missed is greater if a database were searched through this interface than it would be if another interface were searched for the same database.

Despite the fact that these filters will retrieve a number of "false drops," they still limit the number of off-topic references, substantially saving the searcher a great deal of time in reviewing search results.

Just as it is impossible to create a filter that returns only relevant items, it is also impossible to create a filter that *guarantees* complete retrieval of mixed method studies from a particular database. Again, this is because of the lack of standard terminology used to describe mixed method studies. Although some databases have a controlled vocabulary term to represent this method—for example, *CINAHL (Cumulative Index to Nursing & Allied Health Literature)* uses the term "multimethod study" (which the *CINAHL Scope Note* for this term defines as: "Studies which combine quantitative and qualitative methods")—the possibility always exists that a database indexer (the person responsible for assigning subject headings to bibliographic records) will not apply a subject appropriately. At the same time, it is impossible to identify all possible variants of terms authors could use to describe a mixed method study in the abstracts of their articles. Hence, even a carefully constructed search filter may miss references if indexing errors have taken place or if authors use an extremely idiosyncratic way of describing their research. However, the approach taken in these filters should result in a high recall of relevant items with very few, if any, relevant references missed, depending on the topic searched.

How to Use the Filters

After running a subject search for information, the searcher should run a search of the terms contained in the appropriate filter. The results of the subject search should then be combined with the results of the filter search.

If the searcher has an ongoing need to limit searches to mixed methods studies, saving the filter as a "Saved Search" or "Saved History" is suggested. Most database interfaces have a means to save and reexecute search strategies. This normally requires the searcher to create a personal account or profile on the search interface. Those not familiar with saving or reexecuting searches should consult the on-screen Help for the database at hand or ask for assistance from a librarian.

The filters described in this section are reproduced at the following website: http://www.library. ualberta.ca/HealthSciences/MethodologyFilters/index.cfm. Searchers may find it helpful to copy and paste the text from these pages rather than keying in the information directly. When copying the Ovid filters, each numbered line represents a separate search statement and each must be copied separately. Do not include the line numbers that appear to the left of the search statement when copying and pasting. The other filters are contained in a single search statement that can be copied as a whole.

It is important to note that the filters were created on the database interfaces available to the author and these may not necessarily be the same interfaces available to the reader (e.g., *MEDLINE* and *PsycInfo*, in addition to being available via the *OvidSP* interface, are also available on the *EBSCO* interface). If a reader does not have access to a database on the same interface as the filters described below, the filter will have to be adjusted to reflect the search conventions of that interface. The terms will remain the same, but conventions like the field labels, proximity operators, and the requirements for quotes when phrase searching vary from one interface to another. The online Help screens can be consulted to determine the applicable search conventions used with a particular interface. Less experienced searchers may wish to consult a librarian to assist in translating a search filter created for one interface to that of another or if they have any other questions regarding how to use search filters effectively.

Not all of the filters provided are geared to a specific database (e.g., the *EBSCO [Other than CINAHL]*, *CSA Illumina*, *Ovid Textword Search*, and *ProQuest* filters can be used with any database available on that interface). For any databases for which a specific filter is not provided, the searcher should identify the search interface through which he or she accesses the database and select the filter accordingly. For example, if one searcher accesses *ERIC* via the *ProQuest* interface, she or he would use the *ProQuest* filter; if another searcher accesses *ERIC* via *EBSCO*, he or she would use the *EBSCO (Other than CINAHL)* filter.

MEDLINE (OvidSP; Advanced Search)

1. (mixed method* or multiple method* or multi method* or multimethod* or multiple research method* or mixed model* or mixed research).tw.

2. ((qualitative or qual) and (quantitative or quan) and (nested or blend* or concurrent or complementary or expansion or initiation or holistic or transformative or embedded or iterative or triangulat*)).tw.

3. ((quantitative or quan) and (phenomenolog* or ethno* or (grounded adj3 theor*) or hermeneutic* or lived experience* or content analys* or thematic or theme* or narrative* or interview* or focus group* or action research)).tw.

4. (triangulat* adj15 (method* or data or concurrent or sequential or simultaneous or design*)).tw.

5. (qualitative adj5 quantitative adj5 (combin* or mixed or mix or integrat* or method* or analys*)).tw.

6. exp qualitative research/ and quantitative.tw.

7. or/1–6

8. (qualitative and quantitative).tw.

9. exp Nursing Research/ or exp Health Services Research/ or exp Rehabilitation/

10. (px or nu or rh or ed or og or es or eh).fs.

11. (nurs* or educat* or rehabilitat* or psych* or social or socio* or service* or interview* or questionnaire* or survey*).af.

12. or/9–11

13. 8 and 12

14. 7 or 13

15. (clinical trial* or evaluation studies or randomized controlled trial).pt.

16. (randomized or (clinical adj3 trial*) or (controlled adj3 trial*)).mp.

17. 15 or 16

18. qualitative.mp.

19. 17 and 18

20. ((qualitative or quantitative) adj5 nested).tw.

21. 14 or 19 or 20

Search conventions:

- * = truncation
- AdjN = proximity operator e.g., adj5 indicates that terms must appear within five words of each other in any order
- .tw. = search terms in the 'textword' fields, i.e., the Title and Abstract fields of the record
- .af. = search terms in All Fields of the record.
- .pt. = search terms in the Publication Type field.
- .mp. = search the database default fields, in the case of MEDLINE, the title, abstract, subject heading and name of substance field.

- .fs. = search for records containing specified sub-headings
- Exp = term has been 'exploded', i.e., any conceptually narrower term for the subject heading will be included in the search
- / = a slash at the end of a term denotes that it is a controlled vocabulary term (in the case of MEDLINE, it is a MeSH [Medical Subject Heading] term)

EMBASE (OvidSP; Advanced Search)

1. (mixed method* or multiple method* or multi method* or multimethod* or multiple research method* or mixed model* or mixed research).tw.

2. ((qualitative or qual) and (quantitative or quan) and (nested or concurrent or complementary or expansion or initiation or holistic or transformative or embedded or iterative or triangulat*)).tw.

3. ((quantitative or quan) and (phenomenolog* or ethno* or (grounded adj3 theor*) or hermeneutic* or lived experience* or content analys* or thematic or theme* or narrative* or interview* or focus group* or action research)).tw.

4. (triangulat* adj15 (method* or data or concurrent or sequential or simultaneous or design*)).tw.

5. (qualitative adj5 quantitative adj5 (combin* or blend* or mixed or mix or integrat* or method* or analys*)).tw.

6. exp qualitative research/ and quantitative.tw.

7. or/1–6

8. (qualitative and quantitative).tw.

9. (nurs* or educat* or rehabilitat* or psych* or social or socio* or service* or interview* or questionnaire* or survey*).af.

10. 8 and 9

11. 7 or 10

12. (qualitative and (randomized or (clinical adj3 trial*) or (controlled adj3 trial*))).mp.

13. ((qualitative or quantitative) adj5 nested).tw.

14. 11 or 12 or 13

Search Conventions:
- See above under MEDLINE

PsycInfo (OvidSP; Advanced Search)

1. (mixed method* or multiple method* or multi method* or multimethod* or multiple research method* or mixed model* or mixed research).tw.
2. (triangulat* adj15 (method* or data or concurrent or sequential or simultaneous or design*)).tw.
3. (quantitative or quan).tw,md.
4. (phenomenolog* or ethno* or (grounded adj3 theor*) or hermeneutic* or lived experience* or content analys* or thematic or theme* or narrative* or interview* or focus group* or action research).mp.
5. 4 and 3
6. (qualitative.mp. or qualitative study.md.) and (quantitative.mp. or quantitative study.md.)
7. ((qualitative or quantitative) adj5 nested).tw.
8. (qualitative and (randomized or (clinical adj5 trial*) or (controlled adj5 trial*))).tw.
9. or/1–2, 5–8

Search Conventions:

- md. = search terms in the Methodology field
- tw. = search terms in the title, abstract and key concept fields
- See above under MEDLINE for other search conventions

OvidSP Textword Search (Advanced Search)

1. (mixed method* or multiple method* or multi method* or multimethod* or multiple research method* or mixed model* or mixed research).mp.
2. (triangulat* adj5 (method* or data or concurrent or sequential or simultaneous or design*)).mp.
3. (quantitative or quan).mp.
4. (phenomenolog* or ethno* or (grounded adj3 theor*) or hermeneutic* or lived experience* or content analys* or thematic or theme* or narrative* or interview* or focus group* or action research).mp.
5. 4 and 3
6. ((qualitative or qual) and (quantitative or quan).mp.
7. ((qualitative or quantitative) adj5 nested).mp.
8. (qualitative and (randomized or (clinical adj5 trial*) or (controlled adj5 trial*))).tw.
9. 1 or 2 or 5 or 6 or 7 or 8

Search Conventions:
- See above under *MEDLINE*

EBSCO CINAHL

(mixed method* or multiple method* or multi method* or multimethod* or multiple research method* or mixed model* or mixed research) or (MH "Qualitative Studies+" and MH "Quantitative Studies") or (MH Triangulation or method* n3 triangulat* or concurrent n3 triangulat* or triangulat* n3 data or triangulat* n3 sequential or triangulat* n3 simultaneous) or ((phenomenolog* or ethno* or grounded n3 theor* or hermeneutic* or lived experience* or content analys* or thematic or theme* or narrative* or interview* or action research) and quantitative) or (qualitative and quantitative) or (qualitative n5 nested or quantitative n5 nested) or qualitative and (randomized or clinical n5 trial* or controlled n5 trial*)

Search Conventions:

- * = truncation symbol
- MH = MH preceding a term denotes that it is a controlled vocabulary term
- + = a plus symbol following a subject heading indicates that a term has been exploded, i.e., conceptually narrower terms are included
- Nn = proximity operator, e.g., n3 indicates that terms must appear within three words of each other in any order

EBSCO (Other than CINAHL)

(mixed method* or multiple method* or multi method* or multimethod* or multiple research method* or mixed model* or mixed research or triangulat*) or ((phenomenolog* or ethno* or grounded n3 theor* or hermeneutic* or lived experience* or content analys* or thematic or theme* or narrative* or interview* or action research) and quantitative) or (qualitative and quantitative) or (qualitative n5 nested or quantitative n5 nested) or (qualitative and (randomized or clinical n5 trial* or controlled n5 trial*))

Search Conventions:

- See above under *CINAHL*

Web of Science Search (ISI; use the Advanced Search mode)

This database incorporates the following sections: *Science Citation Index*, *Social Sciences Citation Index* and the *Arts & Humanities Citation Index*. Sections can be included/excluded as appropriate to the topic.

TS=("mixed method*" or "multiple method*" or "multi method*" or "multimethod*" or "multiple research methods" or "mixed model*" or "mixed research" or triangulat* same (method* or data or concurrent or sequential or simultaneous or design*) or (quantitative or quan) and (phenomenolog* or ethno* or grounded same theor* or hermeneutic* or "lived experience*" or "content analys*" or thematic or theme* or narrative* or interview* or "focus group*" or "action research") or qualitative and quantitative or qualitative same nested or quantitative same nested or qualitative same randomized or qualitative same clinical same trial* or qualitative same controlled same trial*) or SO=(journal of mixed methods research)

Search Conventions:

- TS = search terms in the title, abstracts and keywords fields of the record
- SO = search terms in the journal name field
- * = truncation
- Same = search terms within the same sentence
- Quotes = required when searching a phrase

SCOPUS (Use the Advanced Search)

(TITLE-ABS-KEY(mixed PRE/0 method*) OR TITLE-ABS-KEY(mixed PRE/0 model*) OR TITLE-ABS-KEY(multi PRE/0 method*) OR TITLE-ABS-KEY(multiple PRE/0 method*) OR TITLE-ABS-KEY("mixed research") OR TITLE-ABS-KEY("multiple research methods") OR TITLE-ABS-KEY(multimethod*)) OR (TITLE-ABS-KEY(triangulat* W/15 method*) OR TITLE-ABS-KEY(triangulat* W/15 data) OR TITLE-ABS-KEY(triangulat* W/15 concurrent) OR TITLE-ABS-KEY(triangulat* W/5 sequential) OR TITLE-ABS-KEY(triangulat* W/15 simultaneous) OR TITLE-ABS-KEY(triangulat* W/15 design)) OR (TITLE-ABS-KEY((quantitative OR quan) AND (phenomenolog* OR ethno* OR grounded same theor* OR hermeneutic* OR "lived experience" OR "lived experiences" OR "content analys*" OR thematic OR theme* OR narrative* OR interview* OR "focus group" OR "focus groups" OR "action research")) OR TITLE-ABS-KEY(qualitative AND quantitative) OR TITLE-ABS-KEY(qualitative W/5 nested) OR TITLE-ABS-KEY(quantitative W/5 nested) OR TITLE-ABS-KEY(qualitative W/15 randomized) OR TITLE-ABS-KEY(qualitative W/15 clinical W/5 trial*) OR TITLE-ABS-KEY(qualitative W/15 controlled W/5 trial*))

Search Conventions:

- * = truncation
- TITLE-ABS-KEY = search terms in the title, abstract and keywords field
- W/n = proximity operator, search terms within N words of each other in any order
- Quotes = required when searching a phrase; however, none of the terms within quotes can be truncated
- PRE/0 = proximity operator used to search an exact phrase when one or more of the words in the phrase has been truncated

CSA Illumina (use the Command Search mode; link available at bottom of Advanced Search page)

(KW=(mixed method* or multiple method* or multi method* or multimethod* or multiple research method* or mixed model* or mixed research or triangulat* or (phenomenolog* or ethno* or grounded theory or hermeneutic* or lived experience* or content analys* or thematic or theme* or narrative* or interview* or action research) and quantitative) or (qualitative and quantitative) or (qualitative within 5 nested or quantitative within 5 nested) or (qualitative and (randomized or clinical within 5 trial* or controlled within 5 trial*)))

Search Conventions:

- * = truncation
- KW = search title, abstracts, descriptor/subject heading and identifier fields
- Within N = proximity operator; search terms within N words of each other in any order

ProQuest

(((mixed method* or multiple method* or multi method* or multimethod* or "multiple research method*" or mixed model* or mixed research or triangulat*) or ((qualitative or quantitative) and nested)) or (qualitative and quantitative)) or (qualitative and (randomized or clinical trial* or controlled trial*))

Search Conventions:
- * = truncation

PubMed

("mixed method" OR "mixed methods" OR "multi method" OR "multi methods" OR "multiple method" OR "multiple methods" OR multimethod OR multimethods OR "mixed model" OR "mixed models" OR "mixed research") OR (qualitative AND quantitative AND (nested OR concurrent OR complementary OR expansion OR initiation OR holistic OR transformative OR embedded OR iterative OR triangulat*)) OR (quantitative AND (phenomenolog* OR ethno* OR "grounded theory" OR hermeneutic* OR "lived experience" OR "lived experiences"OR "content analysis" OR "content analyses" OR thematic OR theme* OR narrative* OR interview* OR "focus group" OR "focus groups" OR "action research")) OR (qualitative AND quantitative AND (combin* OR mixed OR mix OR integrat* OR method OR methods OR methodology OR triangulat* OR analys*)) OR (triangulat* AND (method OR methods OR methodology OR data OR concurrent OR sequential OR simultaneous OR design*)) OR (qualitative research [Mesh] AND quantitative AND (nursing research [mesh] OR health services research [mesh] OR rehabilitation [mesh] OR px[MeSH Subheading] nu[MeSH Subheading] OR rh[MeSH Subheading] Or ed[MeSH Subheading] OR og[MeSH Subheading] OR es[MeSH Subheading] OR eh[MeSH Subheading] OR nurse OR nurses OR nursing OR education OR educational OR rehabilitation OR psychology OR psychological OR psychosocial OR social OR service OR services) OR ((clinical trial OR controlled trial OR randomized OR evaluation studies) AND qualitative) or ((qualitative OR quantitative) AND nested))

Search Conventions:

- * = truncation
- [MeSH] = search term as subject heading; if there are narrower subject headings for the term, they will be included
- [MeSH Subheading] = search for records containing specified sub-headings
- Quotes must be used for textword phrases

References

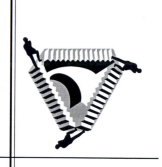

Agar, M. (1996). *The professional stranger: An informal introduction to ethnography*. San Diego, CA: Academic Press.

Anderson, F., Downing, G. M., & Hill, J. (1996). Palliative performance scale (PPS): A new tool. *Journal of Palliative Care, 12*(1), 5–11.

Angrosino, M. (2007). *Participant observation*. Walnut Creek, CA: Left Coast Press.

Atkinson, P., Delamont, S., Coffey, A., Lofland, J., & Lofland, L. (2007). *Handbook of ethnography*. Thousand Oaks, CA: Sage.

Barbour, R. (2007). *Doing focus groups*. Thousand Oaks, CA: Sage.

Bartholomew, K., Henderson, A., & Marcia, J. E. (2000). Coded semistructured interviews in social psychology research In *Handbook of research in social and personality psychology*, H. T. Reis & C. Judd, eds. (pp. 286–321). New York: Cambridge University Press.

Bazeley, P. (2006). The contribution of computer software to integrating qualitative and quantitative data and analysis. *Research in the schools, 13*(1), 64–74.

Bennet, I., Switzer, J., Aguirre, A., Evans, K., & Barg, F. (2006). "Breaking it down": Patient-clinician communication and prenatal care among African American women of low and higher literacy. *Annals of Family Medicine, 4*(4), 334–340.

Bergman, M. M. (ed.). (2008). *Advances in mixed methods research*. Thousand Oaks, CA: Sage.

Bernard, H. R. (2000). *Social research methods*: *Qualitative and quantitative approaches*. Thousand Oaks, CA: Sage.

Booth, W. C., Williams, J. M., & Colomb, G., C. (2003). *The craft of research*, 2nd ed. Chicago: University of Chicago Press.

Borkan, J. (2004). Mixed methods studies: A foundation for primary care research. *Annals of Family Medicine, 2*(1), 4–6.

Bottorff, J. L. (1994). Using videotaped recordings in qualitative research In *Critical issues in qualitative research methods*, J. Morse, ed. (pp. 244–261). Thousand Oaks, CA: Sage.

Bottorff, J. L., & Morse, J. M. (1994). Identifying types of attending: Patterns of nurses' work. *Image: Journal of Nursing Scholarship, 26*(1), 53–60.

Bowers, B., & Schatzman, L. (2008). Dimensional analysis In *Grounded theory: The second generation*, J. M. Morse, P. N. Stern, J. Corbin, B. Bowers, K. Charmaz, & A. Clarke, eds. (pp. 86–106). Walnut Creek, CA: Left Coast Press.

Boyatzis, R. E. (1998). *Transforming qualitative information*. Thousand Oaks, CA: Sage.

Bradburn, N., Sudman, S., & Wansink, B. (2004). *Asking questions: The definitive guide to questionnaire design—For market research, political polls, and social and health questionnaires*. San Francisco: John Wiley & Sons.

Burla, L., Knierim, B., Barth, J., Liewald, K., Duetz, M., & Abel. T. (2008). From text to codings: Intercoding reliability assessment in qualitative analysis. *Nursing Research, 57*(2), 113–117.

Bryman, A. (2006a). *Mixed methods* (Vols. 1–14). London: Sage.

Bryman, A. (2006b). Integrating quantitative and qualitative research: How is it done? *Qualitative Research, 6*(1), 97–113.

Bryman, A. (2007). Barriers to integrating quantitative and qualitative research. *Journal of Mixed Methods Research, 1*(1), 8–22.

Bryman, A. (2008). Why do researchers integrate/combine/mesh/blend/mix/merge/fuse quantitative and qualitative research? In *Advances in mixed methods research*, M. Bergman, ed. (pp. 87–100). London: Sage.

Campbell, M., Fitzpatrick, R., Haines, A., Kinmonth, A. L., Sandercock, P., Spiegelhalter, D., et al. (2000). Framework for design and evaluation of complex interventions to improve health. *British Medical Journal, 321*(7262), 694–696.

Caracelli, V. (2006). Enhancing the policy process through the use of ethnography and other study frameworks: A mixed-method strategy. *Research in the Schools, 13*(1), 84–92.

Charmaz, K. (2006). *Constructing grounded theory: A practical guide through qualitative analysis*. London: Sage.

Charmaz, K. (2008). Shifting the grounds: Constructivist grounded theory methods. In *Grounded theory: The second generation*, J. M. Morse, P. N. Stern, J. Corbin, B. Bowers, K. Charmaz, & A. Clarke, eds. (pp. 127–154). Walnut Creek, CA: Left Coast Press.

Chen, H. T. (2006). A theory-driven evaluation perspective on mixed methods research. *Research in the Schools, 13*(1), 75–83.

Clarke, A. E. (2005). *Situational analysis: Grounded theory after the postmodern turn*. Thousand Oaks, CA: Sage.

Clarke, A. E. (2008). From grounded theory to situational analysis: What's new? Why? How? In *Grounded theory: The second generation*, J. M. Morse, P. N. Stern, J. Corbin, B. Bowers, K. Charmaz, & A. Clarke, eds. (pp. 194–233). Walnut Creek, CA: Left Coast Press.

Corbin, J., & Morse, J. M. (2003). The unstructured interactive interview: Issues of reciprocity and risks. *Qualitative Inquiry, 9*(3), 335–354.

Corbin, J., & Strauss, A. (2008). *Basics of qualitative research*, 3rd ed. Thousand Oaks, CA: Sage.

Côté, J. J., Morse, J. M., & James, S. G. (1991). The pain experience of the post-operative newborn. *Journal of Advanced Nursing, 16*, 378–387.

Creswell, J. W., Fetters, M. D., & Ivankova, N. V. (2004). Designing a mixed methods study in primary care. *Annals of Family Medicine, 2*(1), 7–12.

Creswell, J. W., & Plano Clark, V. L. (2007). *Designing and conducting mixed methods research*. Thousand Oaks, CA: Sage.

Creswell, J. W., Plano Clark, V. L., Gutmann, M. L., & Hanson W. E. (2003). Advanced mixed methods research designs. In *Handbook of mixed methods in social & behavioral research*, A. Tashakkori & C. Teddlie, eds. (pp. 209–204). Thousand Oaks, CA: Sage.

Creswell, J. W., Shope, R., Plano Clark, V. L., & Green, D. O. (2006). How interpretive qualitative research extends mixed methods research. *Research in the Schools, 13*(1), 1–11.

Currall, S. C., & Towler, A. (2003). Research methods in management and organizational research: Toward integration of qualitative and quantitative techniques. In *Handbook of mixed methods in social & behavioral research*, A. Tashakkori & C. Teddlie, eds. (pp. 531–526). Thousand Oaks, CA: Sage.

Curry, L., Shield, R., & Wetle, T. (eds.). (2006). *Improving aging and public health research: Qualitative and mixed methods*. Washington, DC: American Public Health Association.

Dahlberg, K., Nystrom, M., & Drew, N. (2008). *Reflective lifeworld research*, 2nd ed. Lund, Sweden: Studentlitteratur Ab.

Denzin, N. K., & Lincoln, Y. S. (2005). The discipline and practice of qualitative research. In *The Sage handbook of qualitative research*, N. K. Denzin & Y. S. Lincoln, eds. (pp. 1–32). Thousand Oaks, CA: Sage.

Dewar, A., & Morse J. M. (1995). Unbearable incidents: Failure to endure the experience of illness. *Journal of Advanced Nursing, 22*(5), 957–964.

Donavan, J., Mills, N., Smith, M., Brindle, L., Jacoby, A., Peters, T., Frankel, S., Neal, D., & Hamdy, F. (2002). Improved design and conduct of randomized trials by embedding them in qualitative research: ProtecT (Prostate testing for cancer treatment) study. *British Medical Journal, 325*(7367), 766–769.

Eibl-Eibesfeldt, I. (1989). *Human ethology.* New York: Aldine de Gruyter.

Fowler, F. J. (2009). *Survey research methods.* (Applied Social Research Methods Series). Thousand Oaks, CA: Sage.

Glaser, B. G. (1978). *Theoretical sensitivity.* Mill Valley, CA: Sociology Press.

Greene, J. C. (2005). The generative potential of mixed methods inquiry. *International Journal of Research & Method in Education, 28*(2), 207–211.

Greene, J. C. (2006). Toward a methodology of mixed-methods social inquiry. *Research in the Schools, 13*(1), 93–98.

Greene, J. C. (2007). *Mixed methods in social inquiry.* San Francisco: Jossey-Bass.

Greene, J. C., Benjamin, L., & Goodyear, L. (2001). The merits of mixing methods in evaluation. *Evaluation: The International Journal of Theory, Research and Practice, 7*(1), 25–44.

Habashi, J., & Worley, J. (2009). Child geopolitical agency: A mixed methods case study. *Journal of Mixed Methods, 3*(1), 42–64.

Hinton, D. E., Nguyen, L., & Pollack, M. H. (2007). Orthostatic panic events as a key Vietnamese reaction to traumatic events: the case of September 11, 2001. *Medical Anthropological Quarterly, 21*(1), 81–107.

Hodgkin, S. (2008). Telling it all: A story of women's social capital using a mixed methods approach. *Journal of Mixed Method Research, 2*(4), 296–316.

Hroscikoski, M. C., Solberg, L. I., Sperl-Hillen, J. M., Harper, P. G., McGrail, M. P., & Crabtree, B. F. (2006). Challenges of change: A qualitative study of chronic care model implementation. *Annals of Family Medicine, 4*(4), 317–326.

Hsieh, H.-F., & Shannon, S. E. (2005). Three approaches to qualitative content analysis, *Qualitative Health Research, 15*(9), 1277–1288.

Im, E.O., Page, R., Lin, L.C., Tsai, H.M., & Cheng, C.Y.C. (2004). Rigor in cross-cultural nursing research. *International Journal of Nursing Studies, 41,* 891–899.

Johnson, R. B., & Onwuegbuzie, A. J. (2004). Mixed methods research: A research paradigm whose time has come. *Educational Researcher, 33*(7), 14–26.

Johnson, R. B., Onwuegbuzie, A . J., & Turner, L. A. (2007). Toward a definition of mixed method research. *Journal of Mixed Methods Research, 1*(2), 112–133.

Johnstone, P. L. (2004). Mixed methods, mixed methodology health services research in practice. *Qualitative Health Research, 14*(2), 259–271.

Journal of Mixed Methods Research. (2008). About this journal. Retrieved December 17, 2008, from http://www.sagepub.com/journalsProdDesc.nav?prodId=Journal201775

Kieren, D., & Morse, J. M. (1992). Preparation factors and menstrual attitudes of pre- and postmenarcheal girls. *Journal of Sex Education and Therapy, 18,* 155–174.

Kieren, D. K., & Morse, J. M. (1995). Developmental factors and pre- and post-menarcheal menstrual attitudes. *Canadian Home Economics Journal, 45*(2), 61–67.

Kruger, R. (2008). *Focus groups: A practical guide for applied research,* 4th ed. Thousand Oaks, CA: Sage.

Kulig, J. C., Hall, B. I., & Kalischuk, R. G. (2008). Bullying perspectives among rural youth: A mixed-methods approach. *Rural and Remote Health, 8,* 923. (Retrieved from http://www.rrh.org.au, January 6, 2009).

Lehner, P. N. (1979). *Handbook of ethological methods.* New York: Garland STPM Press.

Leventhal, H. (December 1, 1993). *The study of illness cognition from thought to action at the behavioral interface* [videotape]. Gerontology colloquium, Pennsylvania State University.

Locke, L. F., Silverman, S. J., & Spirduso, W. W. (1998). *Reading and understanding research.* Thousand Oaks, CA: Sage.

Maxwell, J. A. (2007). How can "mixed" methods constitute a coherent research strategy? Paper presented at the 6th Congress for Qualitative Inquiry, University of Illinois-Champaign, Illinois, April 2006.

Mayan, M. (2009). *The essentials of qualitative inquiry*. Walnut Creek, CA: Left Coast Press.

Meadows, L., & Morse, J. M. (2001). Constructing evidence within the qualitative project. In *The nature of evidence in qualitative inquiry*, J. M. Morse, J. Swanson, & A. Kuzel, eds. (pp. 187–200). Newbury Park, CA: Sage.

Milburn, K., Fraser, E., Secker, J., & Pavis, S. (1995). Combined methods in health promotion research: Some considerations about appropriate use. *Health Education Journal, 54*(3), 347–356.

Mill, J. E., Jackson, R. C., Worthington, C. A., Archibald, C. P., Wong, T., Myers, T., Prentice, T., & Sommerfeldt, S. (2008). HIV testing and care in Canadian Aboriginal youth: A community based mixed methods study. *BMC Infectious Diseases, 8*, 132.

Miller, R. L., & Brewer, J. D. (eds.). (2003). *The A–Z of Social Research*. Thousand Oaks, CA: Sage.

Morgan, D. G., & Stewart, N. J. (2002). Theory building through mixed-method evaluation of a dementia special care unit. *Research in Nursing & Health, 25*(6), 479–488.

Morgan, D. L. (1998). Practical strategies for combining qualitative and quantitative methods: Applications to health research. *Qualitative Health Research, 8*(3), 362–376.

Morgan, D. L. (September 2004). *Mixed-method design*. Invited keynote address to the 5th Qualitative Research Conference in Health and Social Care, Bournemouthe University, England.

Morse, J. M. (1987). The meaning of health in an inner city community. *Nursing Papers/Perspectives in Nursing, 19*(2), 27–41.

Morse, J. M. (1989). Cultural responses to parturition: Childbirth in Fiji. *Medical Anthropology, 12*(1), 35–44.

Morse, J. M. (1991). Approaches to qualitative-quantitative methodological triangulation. *Nursing Research, 40*(2), 120–123. Reprinted in 2008 in *The mixed methods reader*, V. L. Plano Clark & J. W. Creswell, eds. (pp. 151–160). Thousand Oaks, CA: Sage.

Morse, J. M. (1994). Designing qualitative research. In *Handbook of qualitative inquiry*, Y. S. Lincoln & N. K. Denzin, eds. (pp. 220–235). Menlo Park, CA: Sage.

Morse, J. M. (1999). The armchair walkthrough [Editorial]. *Qualitative Health Research, 9*(4), 435–436.

Morse, J. M. (2001). Toward a praxis theory of suffering. *Advances in Nursing Science, 24*(1), 47–59.

Morse, J. M. (2003). Principles of mixed and multi-method research design. In *Handbook of mixed methods in social and behavioral research*, A. Tashakkori & C. Teddlie, eds. (pp. 189–208). Thousand Oaks, CA: Sage.

Morse, J. M. (2005). Creating a qualitatively-derived theory of suffering. In *Clinical practice and development in nursing*, U. Zeitler, ed. (pp. 83–91). Center for Innovation in Nurse Training, Aarhus, Denmark.

Morse, J. M. (2008). Serving two masters: The qualitatively-driven, mixed-method proposal [Editorial]. *Qualitative Health Research, 18*(12), 1607–1608, DOI: 10.1177/0123456789123456.

Morse, J. M., Beres, M., Spiers, J., Mayan, M., & Olson, K. (2003). Identifying signals of suffering by linking verbal and facial cues. *Qualitative Health Research, 13*(8), 1063–1077.

Morse, J. M., & Carter, B. (1996). The essence of enduring and the expression of suffering: The reformulation of self. *Scholarly Inquiry for Nursing Practice, 10*(1), 43–60.

Morse, J. M., & Doan, H. M. (1987). Growing up at school: Adolescents' response to menarche. *Journal of School Health, 57*(9), 385–389.

Morse, J. M., & Doberneck, B. M. (1995). Delineating the concept of hope. *Image: Journal of Nursing Scholarship, 27*(4), 277–285.

Morse, J. M., Hutchinson, S., & Penrod, J. (1998). From theory to practice: The development of assessment guides from qualitatively derived theory. *Qualitative Health Research, 8*(3), 329–340.

Morse, J. M., & Intrieri, R. (1997). Patient-patient communication in a long-term care facility. *Journal of Psychosocial Nursing & Mental Health Services, 35*(5), 34–39.

Morse, J. M., & Johnson, J. L. (eds.). (1991). *The illness experience: Dimensions of suffering*. Newbury Park, CA: Sage. Online at http://content.lib.utah.edu/u?/ir-main, 2008

Morse, J. M., & Kieren, D. (1993). The Adolescent Menstrual Attitude Questionnaire, Part II: Normative Scores. *Health Care for Women International, 14*, 63–76.

Morse, J. M., Kieren, D., & Bottorff, J. L. (1993). The Adolescent Menstrual Attitude Questionnaire, I: Scale Construction. *Health Care for Women International, 14*, 39–62.

Morse, J. M., & McHutchion, E. (1991). The behavioral effects of releasing restraints. *Research in Nursing and Health, 14*(3), 187–196.

Morse, J. M., & Mitcham, C. (1997). Compathy: The contagion of physical distress. *Journal of Advanced Nursing, 26*, 649–657.

Morse, J. M., & Mitcham, C. (2002). Exploring qualitatively derived concepts: Inductive-deductive pitfalls. In *Issues in validity: Behavioral concepts, their derivation and interpretation*, J. M. Morse, J. E. Hupcey, J. Penrod, J. A. Spiers, C. Pooler, & C. Mitcham, eds., *International Journal of Qualitative Methods, 1*(4), article 3. Retrieved December 15, 2002, from http://www.ualberta.ca/~ijqm

Morse, J. M., Mitcham, C., & van der Steen, V. (1998). Compathy or physical empathy: Implications for the caregiver relationship. *Journal of Medical Humanities, 19*(1), 51–65.

Morse, J. M., & Niehaus, L. (2007). Combining qualitative and quantitative methods for mixed-method designs. In *Nursing research: A qualitative perspective*, 4th ed., P. Munhall, ed. (pp. 541–554). Boston: Jones & Bartlett.

Morse, J. M., Niehaus, L., & Varnhagen, S. (2003). Risks to participants undergoing qualitative interviews: Perspectives of researchers, and research ethics boards [Proposal]. Funded by CIHR, Grant # 11669, J. Morse PI, 2003.

Morse, J.M., Niehaus, L., & Varnhagen, S. (In preparation). The risks inherent in unstructured interview research: An Internet survey.

Morse, J. M., Niehaus, L., & Wolfe, R. (2005). The utilization of mixed-method design in nursing research. *International Nursing Review (Japanese), 28*(2), 61–66.

Morse, J. M., Niehaus, L., Wolfe, R., & Wilkins, S. (2006). The role of theoretical drive in maintaining validity in mixed-method research. *Qualitative Research in Psychology, 3*(4), 279–291.

Morse, J. M., & Penrod, J. (2000). Qualitative outcome analysis: Evaluating nursing interventions for complex clinical phenomena. *Journal of Nursing Scholarship, 32*(2), 125–130.

Morse, J. M., & Proctor, A. (1998). Maintaining patient endurance: The comfort work of trauma nurses. *Clinical Nursing Research, 7*(3), 250–274.

Morse, J. M., Solberg, S., & Edwards, J. (1993). Caregiver-infant interaction: Comforting the postoperative infant. *Scandinavian Journal of Caring Sciences, 7*, 105–111.

Morse, J. M., Stern, P. N., Corbin, J., Bowers, B., Charmaz, K., & Clarke, A. (2008). *Grounded theory: The second generation*. Walnut Creek, CA: Left Coast Press.

Morse, J. M., Swanson, J. M., & Kuzel, T. (2001). *The nature of qualitative evidence*. Thousand Oaks, CA: Sage.

Morse, J. M., Wolfe, R., & Niehaus, L. (2006). Principles and procedures for maintaining validity for mixed-method design. In *Qualitative methods in research and public health: Aging and other special populations*, L. Curry, R. Shield, & T. Wetle, eds. (pp. 65–78). Washington, DC: GSA and APHA.

Olson, K., Krawchuk, A., & Quddusi, T. (2007). Fatigue in individuals with advanced cancer in active treatment and palliative settings [Electronic version]. *Cancer Nursing 30*(4), E1–10.

Olson, K., Hayduk, L., Cree, M., Cui, Y., Quan, H., Hanson, J., Lawlor, P., & Strasser, F. (2008). The causal foundations of variations in cancer-related symptom clusters during the final weeks of palliative care. *BMC Medical Research Methodology 8*, 36.

Olson, K., & Morse, J. M. (2005). Delineating the concept of fatigue using a pragmatic utility approach. In *Essential concepts of nursing*, J. Cutcliff & H. McKenna, eds. (pp. 141–159). Oxford, UK: Elsevier Science.

Olson, K., Morse, J. M., Smith, J., Mayan, M., & Hammond, D. (2000–2001). Linking trajectories of illness and dying. *Omega, 42*(4), 293–308.

Olson, K., Turner, A. R., Courneya, K. S., Field, C., Man, G., Cree, M., & Hanson, J. (2008). Possible links between behavioral and physiological indices of tiredness, fatigue, and exhaustion in advanced cancer. *Supportive Care in Cancer. 16*(3), 251–259.

Onwuegbuzie, A. J., & Johnson, R. B. (2006). The validity issue in mixed research. *Research in the Schools, 13*(1), 48–63.

Onwuegbuzie, A. J., & Teddlie, C. (2003). A framework for analyzing data in mixed methods research. In *Handbook of mixed methods in social & behavioral research*, A. Tashakkori & C. Teddlie, eds. (pp. 351–383). Thousand Oaks, CA: Sage.

Parmelee, J. H., Perkins, S. C., & Sayre, J. J. (2007). "What about people our age?" Applying qualitative and quantitative methods to uncover how political ads alienate college students. *Journal of Mixed Methods Research, 1*(2), 183–199.

Penrod, J., & Morse, J. M. (1997). Strategies for assessing and fostering hope: The *Hope Assessment Guide. Oncology Nurses Forum, 24*(6), 1055–1063.

Pett, M. A. (1997). *Nonparametric statistics for health care research: Statistics for small samples and unusual distributions.* Thousand Oaks, CA: Sage.

Pfefferle, S. G., & Weinberg, D. B. (2008). Certified nurse assistants making meaning of direct care. *Qualitative Health Research, 18*(7), 952–961.

Pincus, Y., Vogel, S., Breen, A., Foster, N., & Underwood, M. (2005). Persistent back pain—Why do physical therapy clinicians continue treatment? A mixed methods study of chiropractors, osteopaths and physio-therapists. *European Journal of Pain, 10*, 67–76.

Plano Clark, V. L., & Creswell, J. W. (2008). *The mixed methods reader.* Thousand Oaks, CA: Sage.

Rea, L. M., & Parker, R.A. (2005). *Designing and conducting survey research: A comprehensive guide*, 3rd ed. San Francisco: Jossey-Bass.

Richards, L. (2005). *Handling qualitative data.* London: Sage.

Richards, L., & Morse, J. M. (2007). *Readme first for a user's guide to qualitative methods*, 2nd ed. Thousand Oaks, CA: Sage.

Richter, K. (1997/2008). Child-care choice in urban Thailand: Qualitative and quantitative evidence of the decisions making process. *Journal of Family Issues, 18*(2), 174–204. Reprinted in *The mixed methods reader*, V. L. Plano Clark & J. W. Creswell, eds. (pp. 550–582). Thousand Oaks, CA: Sage.

Ridenour, C. S., & Newman, I. (2008). *Mixed methods research: Exploring the interactive continuum.* Carbondale: Southern Illinois University Press.

Rocco, T. S., Bliss, L. Gallagher, S., Perz-Prado, A., Alacaci, E., Dwyer, E., Fine, J., & Pappamihiel, N. (2003). The pragmatic and dialectical lenses: Two views of mixed methods used in education. In *Handbook of mixed methods in social & behavioral research*, A. Tashakkori & C. Teddlie, eds. (pp. 595–618). Thousand Oaks, CA: Sage.

Sale, J. E. M., & Brazil, K. (2004). A strategy to identify critical appraisal criteria for primary mixed-method studies. *Quality & Quantity, 38*(4), 351–365.

Sandelowski, M. (2000). Combining qualitative and quantitative sampling, data collection, and analysis techniques in mixed-method studies. *Research in Nursing & Health, 23*(3), 246–255.

Sandelowski, M. (2003). Tales or tableaux? The challenges of writing and reading mixed methods studies. In *Handbook of mixed methods in social & behavioral research*, A. Tashakkori & C. Teddlie, eds. (pp. 321–350). Thousand Oaks, CA: Sage.

Sandelowski, M. (2007). Words that should be seen but not written (Editorial). *Research in Nursing & Health, 30*(2), 129–130.

Sandelowski, M., Voils, C. I., & Barroso, J. (2006). Defining and designing mixed research synthesis studies. *Research in the Schools, 13*(1), 29–40.

Schatzman, L. (1991). Dimensional analysis: Notes on an alternative approach to the grounding of theory in qualitative research. In *Social organization and social process: Essays in honor of Anselm Strauss*, D. Maines, ed. (pp. 303–314). New York: Aldine de Gruyter.

Seigel, S., & Castellan, N. J. (1988). *Nonparametric statistics for the behavioral sciences.* New York: McGraw-Hill.

Solberg, L. I., Crain, A. L., Sperl-Hillen, J. M., Hroscikoski, M. C., Engebreston, K. I., & O'Conner, P. J. (2006). Care quality and implementation of chronic care model: A quantitative study. *Annals of Family Medicine, 4*(4), 310–316.

Solberg, S., & Morse, J. M. (1991). The comforting behaviors of caregivers toward distressed post-operative neonates. *Issues in Comprehensive Pediatric Nursing, 14*(2), 77–92.

Sosu, E. M., McWilliam, A., & Gray, S. (2008). The complexities of teachers' commitment to environmental education: A mixed methods approach. *Journal of Mixed Methods, 2*(2), 169–189.

Spielberg, H. (1975). *Doing phenomenology. Essays on and in phenomenology.* The Hague, Netherlands: Martinus Nijhoff.

Spradley, J. P. (1979). *The ethnographic interview.* New York: Holt, Rinehart and Winston.

Spradley, J. P. (1980). *Participant observation*. New York: Holt, Rinehart and Winston.

Stanczak, G. (2007). *Visual research methods*. Thousand Oaks, CA: Sage.

Stern, P. N. (2008). Glaserian grounded theory. In *Grounded theory: The second generation*, J. M. Morse, P. N. Stern, J. Corbin, B. Bowers, K. Charmaz, & A. Clarke, eds. (pp. 55–65). Walnut Creek, CA: Left Coast Press.

Sussman, A. L., Williams, R. L., Laverence, R., Gloyd, P. W., Jr., & Crabtree, B. F. (2006). The art and complexity of primary care clinicians' preventive counseling decisions: Obesity as a case study. *Annals of Family Medicine, 4*(4), 327–333.

Tashakkori, A., & Teddlie, C. (1998). *Mixed methodology: Combining qualitative and quantitative approaches*. Thousand Oaks, CA: Sage.

Tashakkori, A., & Teddlie, C. (2003). *Handbook of mixed methods in social & behavioral research*. Thousand Oaks, CA: Sage.

Teddlie, C., & Tashakkori, A., (2006). A general typology of research designs featuring mixed methods. *Research in the Schools, 13*(1), 12–28.

Teddlie, C., & Tashakkori, A. (2009). *Foundations of mixed methods research: Integrating qualitative and quantitative approaches in the social and behavioral sciences*. Thousand Oaks, CA: Sage.

Teddlie, C., & Yu, F. (2007). Mixed methods sampling: A typology with examples. *Journal of Mixed Methods Research, 1*(1), 77–100.

Thorne, S. (1994). Secondary analysis of qualitative data: Issues and implications. In *Critical issues in Qualitative Research Methods*, J. Morse, ed. (pp. 263–279). Thousand Oaks, CA: Sage.

Todd, Z., Nerlich, B., McKeown, S., & Clarke, D. (eds.). (2004). *Mixing methods in psychology: The integration of qualitative and quantitative methods in theory and practice*. New York: Psychology Press.

Tukey, J. W. (1977). *Exploratory data analysis*. Reading, MA: Addison-Wesley.

Twinn, S. (2003). Status of mixed method research in nursing. In *Handbook of mixed methods in social & behavioral research*, A. Tashakori & C. Teddlie, eds. (pp. 541–556). Thousand Oaks, CA: Sage.

van Manen, M. (1990). *Researching the lived experience: Human science for an action sensitive pedagogy*. London, Ontario, Canada: Althouse Press.

Wittink, M. N., Barg, F. K., & Gallo, J. J. (2006). Unwritten rules of talking to doctors about depression: Integrating qualitative and quantitative methods. *Annals of Family Medicine, 4*(4), 302–309.

Yin, R. K. (2006). Mixed methods research: Are the methods genuinely integrated or merely parallel? *Research in the schools, 13*(1), 41–47.

Zborowski, M. (1969). *People in pain*. San Francisco: Jossey-Bass.

Index

About the Authors

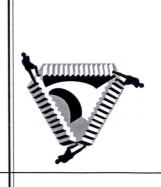

Janice Morse

Janice M. Morse, PhD (Nursing), PhD (Anthropology), FAAN is a professor and Presidential Endowed Chair at the University of Utah College of Nursing and Professor Emeritus, University of Alberta, Canada. She was the founding director and scientific director of the International Institute for Qualitative Methodology, University of Alberta, founding editor for the *International Journal of Qualitative Methods*, and, since 1991, has served as the founding editor for *Qualitative Health Research*. From 1998 to 2007 she was the editor for the Qual Press, and is currently editor for the series *Developing Qualitative Inquiry, The Basics of Qualitative Inquiry* (Left Coast Press) and *Research Programs in Nursing* (Springer). Morse is the recipient of the Episteme Award (Sigma Theta Tau) and honorary doctorates from the University of Newcastle (Australia) and Athabasca University (Canada). She is the author of 350 articles and 15 books on qualitative research methods, suffering, comforting, and patient falls.
janice.morse@nurs.utah.edu

Linda Niehaus

Linda Niehaus has a PhD in Psychology of Education and is a research associate at the University of Alberta, Edmonton, Canada. She completed a Post-Doctoral Fellowship in Qualitative Methods at the International Institute for Qualitative Methodology, University of Alberta. Since 1987, she has been conducting educational, social and health care research, using quantitative, qualitative, and/or mixed methods.

Linda G. Slater

Linda Slater, MLIS, is a librarian with the John W. Scott Health Sciences Library, University of Alberta, Edmonton, Canada, with responsibility for liaison to the University of Alberta Faculty of Nursing. She has advanced expertise in database searching and collaborates frequently with researchers requiring comprehensive literature searches in the area of nursing and related areas.
linda.slater@ualberta.ca